THE 5*th* OPTION

"*The 5th Option* is an outside-the-box look at retirement planning that will help you maximize cash flow and restore peace to your retirement picture. Highly recommended."

—DAVID MCKNIGHT, author of *The Power of Zero*

"*The 5th Option* is a thought-provoking book that takes readers through a true understanding of the different options and approaches they have in securing their retirement. In financial planning, there is not a one-size-fits-all solution for clients' to achieve their dream retirement, but unfortunately many advisors only embrace one approach. What I appreciate most about this book is the manner that the authors identify and simplify additional approaches and share the tradeoffs of each to help readers make well-informed decisions about how they can achieve their ideal retirement."

—DAVE ALISON, CFP®, EA, BPC, chief operating officer and founding partner of C2P Enterprises

"If life was a college course, *The 5th Option* would be required reading. The conversations in this book are poignant and relatable and allow the reader to understand a complex subject. But, more importantly, this book will help you think about retirement planning and your family's financial future differently. *The 5th Option* shows you how to be more efficient with what you have and can have!"

—DR. LAYMON HICKS, speaker, author, and adjunct professor

"Finally, an easy-to-understand book on retirement planning that does the seemingly impossible: The authors successfully marry the investment and life insurance worlds together to create the retirement option every working person needs to know about. *The Fifth Option* is the future of retirement planning!"

—JOHN MONTOYA, founder of JLM Wealth Strategies

"*The 5th Option* inspired us to have new conversations with our financial advisor that provided us with a much more solid understanding of our retirement. In doing so, the stress of the unknown was removed, and we now look forward to those days. We are grateful for how *The 5th Option* positively impacted our lives."

—MIKE DOMITRZ, founder of The Center for Respect and author of *Can I Kiss You?* and *Voices of Courage*

"What a fantastic read! In *The 5th Option*, the authors achieve the rare and difficult feat of telling a compelling story that makes seemingly complex lessons understandable. It's told in the classic 'have some sugar with medicine' style, and the medicine is valuable financial knowledge. This book is a must-read for anyone looking to better understand life's financial journey in the 21st century!"

—JOE FINGERHUT, inspirational keynote speaker and author of *Permission To Play: How Teens Can Build A Life That Is Fun, Fulfilling, and Promising*

"*The 5th Option* offers an eye-opening look at a topic that, while crucial to our future quality of life, is too often sidestepped amidst the busyness of our daily routine. These are solid strategies that are remarkably within our reach and our capabilities. I never knew that there was a 5th Option! This book has set my family on a course for greater financial security and abundance."

—MENDHI AUDLIN, founder of The What If UP Club

"*The 5th Option* is a fun but important read. Being a CFO, I appreciate how this book reinforces the concept of how important cash flow is in retirement. It takes a balanced approach to demonstrating that there are more retirement options than the 4 percent rule, and it explores this rule's limitations. As the title implies, there is a retirement option that fits everyone."

—LYNNETTE FRANK, CPA

"It is such a relief to be able to set up a comprehensive retirement plan that gives such security for the long term! This system allows those of us without a pension, most of us these days, to build our own. It is simple to execute and allows us to sail into retirement without worrying about running out of money! It's a no-brainer!"

—THOMAS MCKENNY, DDS

"If not running out of money and a comfortable retirement are important to you, then this book is a must-read. Retirement planning can be overwhelming; the authors make it easy to understand and provide practical steps you can take today to ensure you have enough to last—comfortably."

—GREGG MAKUCH, chief marketing officer, PTO Exchange

THE 5th
OPTION

THE 5th OPTION

A Journey to Retirement Readiness

Why Your Retirement Plan Won't Work
the Way You Think It Will

WALTER C. YOUNG III, MBA, RICP
and PETER G. BIELAGUS

RIVER GROVE
BOOKS

This book is a critique of several retirement strategies. The information in this book is for general use and while we believe the information is reliable and accurate, it is important to remember individual situations may be entirely different. Therefore, information should be relied upon only when coordinated with individual professional tax and/or financial advice from properly licensed professionals. You need to consider your specific situation, including your health and legacy goals, before acting on any information presented in this book. Please note that neither the information presented nor any opinion expressed is to be considered as an offer to buy or purchase any insurance or securities products and services referenced in this book.

The information provided is not intended to be tax, financial, or legal advice. Individuals are encouraged to seek advice from their own tax and legal counsel. They are also encouraged to seek advice from their own financial and/or insurance professional.

This publication is designed to provide accurate and authoritative information in regard to the subject matter covered. It is sold with the understanding that the publisher and authors are not engaged in rendering legal, accounting, or other professional services. Nothing herein shall constitute legal advice or a solicitation to offer legal advice. If legal advice or other expert assistance is required, the services of a competent professional should be sought.

This book is a work of fiction. Names, characters, businesses, organizations, places, events, and incidents are either a product of the author's imagination or are used fictitiously. Any resemblance to actual persons, living or dead, events, or locales is entirely coincidental.

Published by River Grove Books
Austin, TX
www.rivergrovebooks.com

Distributed by River Grove Books

Design and composition by Greenleaf Book Group
Cover design by Greenleaf Book Group and Mimi Bark
Cover Image: time and money with white background, used under license from Shutterstock.com

Publisher's Cataloging-in-Publication data is available.

Hardcover ISBN: 978-1-63299-411-0

Paperback ISBN: 978-1-63299-409-7

eBook ISBN: 978-1-63299-410-3

First Edition

To the four that make the five fabulous.

—Walter C. Young III

*To my niece, Lilly, by the time you retire may
the financial problems outlined in this book be no more.*

—Peter G. Bielagus

CONTENTS

NOTE TO READER

Personal finance. Corporate finance. Both fields share the same word—*finance*—but they manifest themselves in completely different ways.

I've had the pleasure of studying and working in both fields. After I received my MBA, I worked for a major leading worldwide consulting firm, helping companies design and implement various corporate strategies. After several years consulting in the corporate world, I moved into the world of personal finance. I completed the Retired Income Certification Program, RICP®, (among others) and spent many years helping individuals design and implement their personal financial strategies.

The opportunity to study and work in designing and implementing both corporate and personal strategies provided me with a unique perspective. A perspective that became the impetus of this book. I began to wonder: *What if corporate finance and personal finance share more than just the word* finance?

For the most part, corporate finance is focused on maximizing shareholders' value; squeezing every ounce of efficiency to get the owners of corporations the profits they expect. Corporate finance likes to measure earnings, profits, and cash flow.

On the other hand, personal finance focuses on saving big piles of money to pay for expensive items, like cars, houses, and college educations. Of course, the main thrust of personal finance is to accumulate a pile of money big enough to pay for the most expensive item of all—retirement.

Personal finance focuses on investing money in special accounts designed to help the investor grow their money. These accounts have different names, different purposes, and different advantages—401k, Roth IRA, 529, and more. Most retirement planning revolves around putting dollars into a tax-deferred account, letting that account grow as large as possible, and then, upon retirement, slowly withdrawing from that account.

When I began working in the field of personal finance, I quickly realized a fatal flaw in the strategy of accumulating large piles of money to pay for lifestyle choices and to fund retirement. While many households may not be able to identify the problem, they certainly can *feel* it. One need look no further than the average American family struggling to fund their retirement. Over the years, people have shared their frustrations with me. They feel they are playing a game they can't win.

The bad news is that, in large part, they are right. They *can't* win the personal finance game the way they are doing it.

The good news, for my clients and now for you, dear reader, is that my *corporate* experience provided the solution.

What if every household ran as a small business, with the family members as shareholders? Wouldn't families also want to maximize the value of their household just as Wall Street does? After all, doesn't every household also have assets and liabilities? Income and expenses? Tax planning just like corporations?

Personal finance has been a volume game based on how many dollars you can save, whereas corporate finance sets up cash flow though efficiencies. This is a significant weakness in personal finance, a weakness I have pledged to help change. When we educate individuals to focus on cash flow instead of accumulating as many dollars as possible, retirement dreams happen.

That is my mission.

* * *

What follows is a story about retirement planning as well as a critique of several popular retirement strategies. While there is no "best strategy"—each of us needs to evaluate retirement options and strategies based on our own unique situation and preferences—what they all have in common is a new way to look at one retirement planning option—namely what we—the authors—describe as the Fifth Option.

Through the lens of storytelling, *The Fifth Option* illustrates a familiar path on which many retirees find out just how ill-prepared they are for retirement. They'll discover:

- just how little income they are positioned to enjoy in retirement

- the level of frustration they will endure to try to avert a disappointing retirement

The Fifth Option will take you along as Michael and Jill Cunningham learn they are no different from many other would-be retirees. The characters aren't real, but their problems are. The couple will come to understand how they got to this juncture despite following common financial advice. Their guide, Edward, will provide a bit of historical context as well as a critique of various retirement strategies so you and our couple can really appreciate how most of us share the same predicament.

Slowly and methodically, Michael and Jill will begin to see that their reduced retirement plans *can* have a future—one that is rooted in the latest retirement research, which exposes the serious faults of traditional retirement planning.

We want you to know that because this book is in story form, we have

taken out some of the more technical aspects and rigor of a normal retirement analysis. We have simplified items like taxes and inflation, among
other considerations. Where possible, we use historical returns of the S&P
for context. Why? We wanted the concepts to come to the fore, rather than
more complicated math, which can be a distraction.

For those readers used to mathematical analyses, we understand that
our decision might be frustrating, but in our experience once the concepts
are truly understood, the math falls into place. For the data lovers out
there, we have cited the appropriate studies where applicable.

And of course, every book of this nature needs a statement like this:
*No component of the book is meant to act as any kind of recommendation,
advice, or formal financial plan. Please consult a qualified professional before
taking any kind of action.*

If at the end of the book you are as moved as many of my clients are
when they first learn about the Fifth Option, I will gladly offer a path to
explore this more fully with you.

—Walter C. Young III, MBA, RICP

ACKNOWLEDGMENTS

Writing my first book certainly has been a memorable adventure. As with all efforts born out of passion it took on a life of its own. When Peter Bielagus agreed to be my copilot on this journey, I knew he would have the patience for us to explore the topic, the discipline to keep us moving, and the resolve to see us through. His insights, creativity, and compelling style have made this process enjoyable.

A special thanks goes out to Jason L. Smith, founder of Clarity 2 Prosperity and of the JL Smith Group in Ohio, for his permission to use the methodology from his book, *The Bucket Plan: Protecting and Growing Your Assets for a Worry-Free Retirement*. Jason is an industry thought leader dedicated to the education and success of retirees. His insight and generosity have made a significant impact on my practice as well as on the practices of countless other advisors he works with. If you have not read his book, I highly encourage you to do so.

I also want to acknowledge that many of the concepts and analogies in this book are the results of financial planning giants too numerous to thank. So many will benefit because of your selfless dedication, willingness to share ideas, and impactful research. You have begun a movement to bring about new retirement strategies in a time of great need.

—Walter C. Young III, MBA, RICP

* * *

Six months before I typed this sentence, a longtime friend asked me if I would coauthor a book on a new type of retirement strategy. I had written three books on personal finance, but I was looking for something new and different. Not only was the strategy that the book presented a novel one, so was the idea of writing with a coauthor.

In my coauthor, Walter Young, I couldn't have found a better teammate, and I am honored that Walter asked me to join him in this endeavor.

A book is built by many workers: Thanks go to Andrew Roberts, my most loyal reader, and a man who is the perfect balance of artist and engineer. To my other readers, thank you for your open and honest feedback. To my literary agent, Ken Atchity, who has been with me from the beginning and who believed in me when few others did. To my awesome network of friends who have helped me build a speaking career that has taken me all over the world teaching personal finance. To my family, who are, and always will be, my rock—Mom, Dad, Ryan, Jackie, Mei Ling, Justin, Lily, and now baby Alexis—I love you all very much.

—Peter G. Bielagus

INTRODUCTION

On May 24, 1543, in the small town of Frombork, Poland, a mathematician lay on his deathbed and wondered if now was the time to let go of his secret. He was, by all measures, an important man, but his death would catapult him to eternal fame. For only his death could free him from the dangers of revealing the idea behind his lifelong research. The Greeks had surfaced the idea some 18 centuries earlier, but its boldness was so great that the concept had been forced into hibernation for more than a thousand years. Inevitably, scientific progress unearthed the truth once again, and its acceptance was tested. After the man's death, however, and despite conclusive proof, the idea did not immediately take hold as scientific fact. It took another century before the community at large accepted the theory.

The mathematician was Nicolaus Copernicus, and according to legend, he was in a coma shortly before his death with a faithful protégé nearby. When Copernicus suddenly awoke from his coma, the faithful protégé surprised his teacher with the manuscript Copernicus had completed some 10 years earlier. The manuscript, as the world now knows, challenged the popular conventional model of the universe—that the sun revolved around the earth—and proposed a heliocentric model instead. Copernicus proved that the earth revolves around the sun.

Copernicus saw the manuscript and was filled with joy knowing his life's work would finally be published. The story ends with his living just long enough to see the manuscript go to print so that his lifelong research could be shared with the world.

What Copernicus did not know was that his idea of the earth's revolving around the sun was so controversial that it would take another 100 *years* for the world to accept it as fact. Only with the aid of Sir Isaac Newton was the idea finally pushed to the forefront of the scientific community. While the story of Nicolaus Copernicus and his reluctance to withhold his findings can teach us many things, perhaps chief among them is that established ideas are hard to change. Challenging the norm comes with, well, challenges. Those who benefit from the status quo will fight hard to prevent any real change.

But this is not a book about a Renaissance-era mathematician or celestial revolutions. This is a book about contemporary retirement planning. What is the connection you might ask?

For almost half a century, retirement planning has been governed by a simple premise: Save as much money as possible in a tax-favored retirement account. Upon retirement, systematically withdraw money from that account. This conventional retirement thinking began in the late 1970s and has grown to become the most common retirement strategy.

But times have changed over the last 50 years. Interest rates are at historic lows. Life expectancies are longer than ever. The markets have performed—both up *and* down—in ways never seen before. The way *to* retirement is no longer the way *through* retirement.

Yes, times have changed. Will you change with them?

The financial world is facing a challenge as bold as Copernicus's challenge to the astronomical world. It is part of a new way of thinking that will affect the lives of tens of millions of Americans, their children, and, one day, their grandchildren. In the retirement world, two forces have been battling for nearly half a century, struggling for preeminence. It's a battle mostly unknown to the general public; but the financial world, with its mutual funds, stocks and bonds, and the insurance world, with its own bundle of products, have been at war. Each side has been arguing to millions of consumers that *they* alone have the solution to a client's retirement dreams. Two opposite schools of thought, each filled with intelligent people making convincing arguments, have been battling it out in offices, on phone calls, and at kitchen tables.

Sadly, as the battle has dragged on, the heaviest casualties have fallen not on the insurance or financial side but on the retiree. For almost a half-century the arguments have carried on, largely unchallenged, just like the geocentric model that the earth was the center of the solar system. In the ancient world, science suffered until the truth was accepted. In the modern world, it's the retiree who is at risk.

But just as Copernicus's idea finally won acceptance 100 years after its publication, so too are the financial and insurance worlds beginning to change. And the change started much in the same way—by asking a simple question:

"What if the financial and insurance worlds worked *together*?"

CHAPTER 1

THE SANTA CLAUS MEETING

"How did it go?"

Kathleen Cunningham West hardly had to ask. She could tell from the look on their faces. For a moment, she smiled to herself.

It wasn't so long ago when I had that look.

She stepped aside as her brother and sister-in-law took off their coats. "I take it things didn't go well?"

"Wine first." Michael Cunningham gave his sister a hug and handed her a bottle of cabernet.

"Michael and I could use a glass." Jill Cunningham offered a second hug.

"Well, make yourselves comfortable, and I'll be right back. Then I want to hear about it."

Moments later, they were sitting around the glass coffee table in the Wests' living room. Michael and Jill took the couch, while Kathleen and her husband, Paul, occupied the easy chairs.

Ever since Michael and Jill had moved closer to Kathleen and her husband, the two couples had held a monthly dinner party. Despite careers and kids, they had done a pretty good job of maintaining the plan. This month's dinner was at the Wests' home, and the ritual within the ritual was the predinner drink in the living room.

Michael and Jill had just come from a meeting with their longtime financial advisor. His office was on the way to the Wests' home, so the pair had often stopped to check in on their retirement progress. Normally, the meetings were simple confirmations that the Cunninghams were doing everything right. Normally, Michael and Jill arrived in good cheer, confident the plan they had set in motion long ago would one day pay off.

But something had happened at this day's meeting, and Kathleen Cunningham West had a pretty good guess as to what it was.

Drinks in hand, she opened the discussion: "So what happened?"

"Well," Jill began, "it started off like every other meeting. Our advisor told us our investments are doing well. Our portfolio is growing, and he complimented us for being good, consistent savers. In fact, we are on track to have even *more* saved up than we thought. But since we're not getting any younger, we wanted to focus less on how big our portfolio is and more on what happens next."

Paul leaned forward. "What did you ask?"

"We wanted to get a sense of our retirement lifestyle. I asked what I thought would be a simple question: 'Based on the returns we have been averaging, will our retirement incomes be roughly the same as our incomes now?'" Jill sipped her wine.

"And I wanted to see how our advisor's projections about our retirement income matched up to my own projections," Michael added. "But when I told him what my projections were, he looked at me like I had two heads."

"When he turned his monitor toward us," Jill went on, "Michael and I just stared in disbelief. His numbers were almost *half* of what we had calculated."

"Well, how did you reach *your* projections, baby bro?" Kathleen asked.

"Simple," Michael said. "We've been earning a great average return over the last 15 years. If we can continue to earn that same average return during retirement, I thought that as long as we take out *less* than the aver-age, we are on track to have a *great* retirement income."

"So, for example," Kathleen said, "if you were averaging 8 percent per year on your investments, as long as you withdraw *less* than 8 percent a year, things would be looking good?"

"Exactly. Things look very good," Michael said.

"Then what was the problem?" Kathleen feigned confusion.

"Evidently there are a lot of problems," Michael replied.

"I guess we don't really understand how retirement planning works," Jill added, the sarcasm dripping from her voice.

"First our advisor reminded us we don't have pensions," Michael said. "I felt like saying, 'Hello, we know that!' But I let him talk. He said people without pensions need to fund retirement all by themselves. That, he told us, makes it harder. Then he rattled off the usual suspects that every finan-cial advisor talks about. Like inflation."

"Higher taxes . . . "

"Rising health-care costs. And . . . well, I'm sure there were others, but at this point my head was spinning."

"Then get this," Jill gestured with her hands, nearly spilling her cabernet on the plush white carpet. "He says, 'But all those concerns aren't really the *big* concerns.' So naturally we asked, 'What are the big concerns then?'"

Michael jumped in, "He said the first big concern is that the markets can be volatile. I told him we get that. We've been investing in the markets for more than 15 years. The markets are volatile; they go up and down. We get it. We're comfortable with some volatility. Like I said, we've been earning a great average return."

The oh-so-misleading-average-rate-of-return, Kathleen thought to her-self. *I used to think that's how it worked. Boy, was I wrong.* But she held her tongue. People didn't change their minds from one conversation. "So what did your advisor say to that?" she asked.

"He said that average rates of return need to be viewed differently during retirement. So I pulled out my spreadsheet and showed it to him.

I asked him, 'What's wrong with assuming that if we keep averaging 8 percent a year on our portfolio, and we continue to withdraw LESS than 8 percent per year, we'll be fine?' I asked him why that wouldn't work."

Paul eased back in his chair and crossed his ankles. "And what did he say?"

"He didn't really answer us," Jill said. "He just put on his 'lawyer' cap and said that past results are no guarantee of future returns. And he repeated that volatility and average rates of return need to be treated differently in retirement. He said because of that we will probably need to be super conservative with how much money we withdraw from our retirement account every year."

"Before we could ask him to explain," Michael jumped in, "he told us the other big concern."

"What was that?" Kathleen asked, although she already knew the answer.

"He asked us to guess how long we were going to live," Jill held up her glass. "Well, here's to 100 years."

"Seriously, how are we supposed to know that?" Michael asked. "Dad's in his 80s. Mom passed away in her 70s. Jill's father is 84, and her mother passed at 82. We both have aunts who are in their 90s. But what does all that mean for us?"

"What did he say?" Kathleen asked. Again, she already knew the answer.

"He said the reason he asked was because he has this fancy financial planning software that estimates a person's income when they retire," Jill said. "One of the inputs he needs is how long we think we will live. Of course we have no clue how long we are going to live, so the input is kind of a joke."

"But we played along, and we guessed we'd live until we were 90," Michael said. "Then I asked him where he was going with all this."

"And that," Jill held up her wine glass, "is when he turned his monitor around and showed us a retirement income way less than we expected."

"He must have seen our jaws drop because he immediately told us we can live on more, but we need to be comfortable with a higher chance of our plan not working."

"That's where I almost lost it," Jill said. "I didn't even know what he meant by that. So I asked him point blank, 'What do you mean by *not working*?'"

"He told us," Michael said, "that in the retirement world, 'not working' simply means we run out of money before we die. He said if we are comfortable with an 80 percent chance of success, we could take out more income."

"An 80 percent chance of success means we *also* need to be comfortable with a 20 percent chance of *failure*!" Jill added. "I mean, all we've been doing, all the sacrificing, all that was for a *one-in-five* chance we might run out of money? Are you kidding me? I'm not comfortable with *any* level of failure!"

"Well, we sure as heck don't want to run out of money," Michael went on. "So we asked him how much money we can take out and be *sure* we won't be broke."

"I take it you didn't like his answer?" Paul asked.

"Not. At. All." Jill raised her wine glass to sip.

"He said if we did not live to age 90 but closer to the average life expectancy, we could take out more income."

Jill lowered her glass without drinking. "I was like, *seriously*? The sooner we die the more fun we can have? He didn't say that, but literally, that's what he was saying."

Michael sighed. "He said today's retirement planning has no real guarantees to it, so it's really about getting comfortable with the chance of running out of money. I couldn't follow him on what that means, but our advisor said it's basically a three-way tug of war between how long we *think* we will live, versus how much money we want to withdraw every year, versus how comfortable we are with the risk that we might run out of money."

> Our advisor said it's basically a three-way tug of war between how long we *think* we will live, versus how much money we want to withdraw every year, versus how comfortable we are with the risk that we might run out of money.

Michael stared into his glass. "He painted two very different scenarios for us—one where we lived for a long time but could take out very little money and another where we lived a very short time but could take out a lot more money."

"So I said we want the scenario where we live a long time *and* take out a lot of money. And he said we could do that, but *that* scenario had a very high chance of failure."

"It appears," Michael added, "that the longer we think we will live, the less money we can take out. And if we want to take out more money, then we have to accept a bigger chance we will run out of money during our retirement."

> The longer we think we will live, the less money we can take out. And if we want to take out more money, then we have to accept a bigger chance we will run out of money.

"There was no combination we liked," Jill said. "Where is the combination where we have little chance of failure *and* the income we want, *regardless* of how long we live?"

"Or how about *no* chance of failure?" Kathleen said.

"Exactly, Kath. But I don't know if that option even exists." Michael downed the rest of his wine and set the glass on the edge of the coffee table. "I felt like all our sacrificing doesn't matter. If this is what our retirement will be like, a never-ending guessing game of life expectancy, income level, and chance of failure, then what's the point?"

Kathleen nodded as the room fell silent. It wasn't so long ago that she and Paul had learned from their own advisor about just how little money a retiree could withdraw.

"So, what did you say to your advisor?" she asked.

"We told him we want more income than that," Michael said.

"Like twice as much!" Jill cried. "I thought about all the things Michael and I had planned for our retirement. We wanted to take that cruise to the Caribbean. And we wanted to spend a month in Hawaii, revisiting all the places we visited on our honeymoon. When we're not working, we want to volunteer more with our charities. And what if the kids move away after college? We want to have the funds to visit them."

"And I've been looking forward to getting my golf handicap under 15," Michael said.

"That will definitely require a lot of expensive lessons," Kathleen joked. There was a short burst of laughter, then Paul spoke. "So what did your advisor suggest?" Paul glanced at his wife.

Michael removed a small notebook from his back pocket, and Kathleen smiled. In this ever-growing technological world, her brother still carried around a pocket notebook. Michael thumbed to a page. "Here were his suggestions on how we can increase our retirement income." Michael cleared his throat. "Option One: Work longer." He glanced up from his notebook and explained, "With the stress of our jobs, we're not into that."

"Annnnd," Jill chimed in, "how *much* longer? Another year? Five more years?"

"Option Two," Michael looked around the room, "give up some, or even *all*, of our retirement dreams. Equally as terrible as Option One."

"Option Three," Jill said, "take on more risk, to hopefully get a better return."

"Keyword there being *hopefully*," Kathleen said.

"That's right." Michael turned a page in his notebook. "And that, ladies and gentlemen, brings us to the ultra-unattractive Option Four. Save. More. Money."

He closed his notebook and tapped it on his knee. "If we want to reach our goals, those are our four options."

"Work longer, retire on less, risk more, or save more." Paul ticked the choices off on his fingers. "So, which one are you going to go with?"

"Well, we don't like any of them," Jill said. "I mean who would? All of them demand we sacrifice more, but sacrificing is what we've *already* been doing. Now suddenly, we find out it is not enough."

"And I *still* don't entirely understand why it won't work," Michael said. "We've been doing everything that our advisor suggests. We're great savers. We regularly contribute to our retirement accounts. And we've been averaging great returns. Now to be told it may not be enough, well it's . . . it's just infuriating."

We're great savers. We regularly contribute to our retirement accounts. And we've been averaging great returns. Now to be told it may not be enough, well it's . . . it's just infuriating.

Kathleen smiled at her husband. Then she turned to her brother. "Sounds like you and Jill just had the 'Santa Claus meeting.'"

Michael cocked his head. "The what?"

"That's what I called it when it happened to us three years ago. You go on for years believing your retirement plan is hunky-dory, then in one meeting, you find out it is not. It's just like the day you learned the truth about Santa Claus. It feels like a betrayal, doesn't it? Everything you were told turns out to be false."

"I guess you're right, Kath," Michael said. "But obviously, we have to do something."

Paul winked at Kathleen. "So, again, which option are you going with?"

"Honestly, Paul, we'll probably have to do a little of everything," Jill said. "A little here, a little there."

Michael turned to his sister with a more serious tone. "Kath, Jill, and I were talking. One thing we could cut is that whole-life insurance policy that Dad pretty much forced us to buy when we got married. If we canceled that policy and just got term insurance, we would have a lot more money to put toward retirement."

Kathleen nodded.

Michael smiled at her and held up his hand. "Yeah, yeah, I know what you're going to say, sis." Doing his best dad imitation, he recounted the words that had been drilled into his sister and him. "The whole-life policy is with me my whole life. And I know it builds up a cash value."

"It does a lot more than that, baby bro. For one, whole-life insurance allows you . . . "

"It doesn't matter what it can do, Kath," Michael interrupted. "Those policies are just too expensive."

"The bottom line is that Michael and I need to be more aggressive," Jill said. "The cash value of the life insurance is nice, but it just doesn't grow fast enough."

Kathleen smiled inside. Then she looked at her watch.

"Tell you what. Dinner is just about ready, and I, for one, am starving. Let's eat and no more talk about retirement. Deal?"

"Deal," Michael and Jill agreed.

* * *

When the meal was finished, and all the plates were cleared and cleaned, Michael and Jill retrieved their coats from the front hall and said their goodbyes. As they stepped outside, Kathleen stood in the doorway and spoke. "Michael, if you and Jill feel the best course for your retirement is to cancel your whole-life insurance policies, then I think you should do that. But I think you owe it to Dad to tell him that in person. You know that those policies were important to him. I am heading up to see him tomorrow. Maybe you want to tag along?"

Michael buttoned his coat as he considered his sister's idea. He hadn't been planning on visiting their father this weekend, but she had a point. Their father had insisted they buy those policies. Now after eight years of payments, they were about to let them go, and the old man was entitled to an in-person explanation. He bit his lip. "If we go up there, is Dad going to draft us as free labor to paint the barn?"

Kathleen turned up her hands. "Ya got me. How about I pick you up at nine?"

Michael looked at his wife, who confirmed that would work.

"Okay, nine it is. Thanks again for dinner, Kath. It was great."

"Anytime."

Michael and Jill turned to go.

When Michael was halfway to his car, Kathleen called out, "Michael, you wrote down the options your advisor offered to ensure you had the retirement you hoped for. What were they again?"

Michael cocked his head, then decided to play along. In an elevated voice he recounted, "Option One—work longer. Option Two—get rid of some or even all of our retirement dreams. Option Three—take on more risk. Option Four—save more money."

Michael looked up to see his sister's arms uncrossed and her right hand held up with four extended fingers as she counted his four options. Her thumb was conspicuously tucked in.

"Okay," Kathleen said. "Now write this down."

He opened his notebook to the next blank page and waited.

"What if there is a better way?" Kathleen said.

Michael smiled up at her. "What do you mean?"

Kathleen extended her thumb. "What if there was a fifth option?"

Michael's Notebook:

- Problems with retirement planning:
  ◊ Longer life expectancies
    — Will we live 3 more years or 30? (Don't know so have to plan for 30.) Need to be *super* cautious.
- Volatility of markets
    — Why is this different during retirement?
    — I average an 8 percent return per year. I take out 7 percent per year. Advisor says this won't work. WHY???
- Why isn't average rate of return the same in retirement?
- Big concerns with retirement planning:
    — The higher the retirement income (withdrawals), the higher the chance of failure.
    — The lower the retirement income (withdrawals), the lower the chance of failure.
    — What level of failure are we comfortable with?
- Four options to improve our chances of a successful retirement:
  ◊ **Option One:** Work longer. (But how much longer?)
  ◊ **Option Two:** Get rid of some, or even all, of our retirement dreams. (How is this creating a MORE successful retirement?)
  ◊ **Option Three:** Take on more risk. (What if that backfires and we wind up with even **less** money?)
  ◊ **Option Four:** Save more money? (HOW??? Possibly cut whole-life policy and switch to term?)
- There has GOT to be a better way.
- **What is the Fifth Option???**

CHAPTER 2

CRACKS IN THE NEST EGG

M ichael appreciated his sister's offer to drive. The family farm was an hour outside their New England suburb, and the trip gave him a chance to clear his mind. His sister, the ever-prescient sibling, knew he needed the silence. He stared out the window at the crisp fall scenery. Slowly, the strip malls and subdivisions gave way to cornfields. Michael laid his head back on the headrest and thought about how things had come to this.

Less than 24 hours had passed since that fateful meeting with their financial advisor. One minute he was proud of the savings he and Jill had accumulated. He counted his wife and himself among the ranks of diligent, disciplined investors. But in one meeting, that all had unraveled.

What frustrated him even more was the fact that he still didn't understand *why* his retirement plan wouldn't add up the way he thought it would. Why was there such a difference in outcomes if they lived longer? As long as they kept earning their average rate of return, wouldn't their retirement fund grow? Why *couldn't* a person just take out slightly less than their average yearly return? If a person averaged 8 percent a year, why couldn't they take out 7 percent? Or if they earned 7 percent, why couldn't they take out 6 percent? Sure, there were unknown factors. There always were. That's why a person took out *less* than their average rate of return. There was no reason for their retirement income to be the low number their advisor suggested. It just didn't make sense.

What frustrated him even more was the fact that he still didn't understand *why* his retirement plan wouldn't add up the way he thought it would. Why was there such a difference in outcomes if they lived longer?

Frustrated, he tried to focus his thoughts on a happier subject.

It had been a few months since Michael had seen his father. They had come down for the summer bringing the kids for a long weekend with his dad. He was grateful that he and Jill got along with his father. The visit had been a warm and enjoyable experience. And everyone had stuck to the two cardinal family rules—no politics and no finances.

Today, however, Michael and Kathleen were traveling to their father's house to break one of those very rules. Michael had had only one financial talk with his father. It was years ago, just after he and Jill got married. They had been contributing to their employers' retirement plans, and Michael's father confirmed this was a good idea.

But he made one request from his son and new daughter-in-law. Michael's father had pretty much insisted that they each get permanent insurance policies. Now that they were married, it was time to get serious about life insurance beyond the small term policies from their employers' benefits packages.

The policies his dad advocated, Michael knew, lasted a person's whole life, unlike less expensive term policies. Whole-life policies also built up a cash value. While the cash value was a nice addition, it did come at a price. Whole-life policies could be much more expensive than term insurance.

Michael's father had argued passionately for the whole-life option. His father loved to say, "I've spent my whole life arguing for whole life."

Edward Russell Cunningham had started his career as a life insurance agent. Although he never talked much about work, he'd been in the business 30 years and had seen his share of downturns: the crash of '87, the dot-com debacle, the mortgage crisis. Throughout these highs and lows, Edward would mention to Michael how glad his clients were that they had their whole-life policies.

Michael respected his father and the success he had enjoyed throughout his career, but he felt that whole-life insurance wouldn't work in the modern world. Today a person had to save an enormous amount of money for retirement. The cash value of the whole-life policies simply didn't grow fast enough to keep up with the markets. Today a person needed to focus on *investments*—market-based financial vehicles that had the power to grow a nest egg.

Today a person needed to focus on *investments*—market-based financial vehicles that had the power to grow a nest egg.

Michael appreciated the need for life insurance, and he could see the value of the piggy bank safety cushion inherent in whole-life policies. He had to admit that his father and mother had done quite well. They had seen their share of ups and downs, and they had always come out okay.

But life insurance was the *old* way of saving for retirement. After this last meeting with their advisor, the high premiums seemed an expense they could no longer afford. Their whole-life policies inhibited their retirement growth. At the time of purchase, Michael had had an inkling the policies would be a problem, but his father's insistence persuaded him to ignore that hunch.

Buy these and thank me later, his father had said.

Well, later has arrived, Michael thought. If he and Jill wanted to have the retirement of their dreams they *had* to save more money. They couldn't work any harder, and they had already cut back as much as they could. They needed to save more, and their advisor was right. The insurance premiums they paid each month seemed a likely target. If they canceled the policies and replaced them with lower-premium term policies, they would have a good deal of money they could plow into their retirement accounts. The policies had to go.

Michael saw the familiar pond, barely big enough for a family of ducks, that marked the far corner of the farm. He grinned at the word. The family "farm" was really a 10-acre lot surrounded by actual working farms. But during Michael and Kathleen's childhood, it had been their weekend escape to the country. They had grown corn on part of the property, and they raised chickens and goats and even had a horse for several years. Even if it wasn't technically a farm, the place had given him many happy memories.

Michael stirred in his seat and thought about the conversation he was about to have with his father. He pulled out his notebook and jotted some discussion points.

Michael's Notebook:

- The advisor says we can only take out a very small amount of our retirement savings per year. Much smaller than I thought. (Still don't understand why.) That's not enough. We need a bigger nest egg and for that **we need growth**.

- We need to save more money. Easiest way is to cancel whole-life policies, replace with lower-premium term policies. Insurance coverage would be the same.

- Difference in premiums we would invest in the markets.

- Cash value of life insurance grows, but markets grow faster.

CHAPTER 3

B.S. RETIREMENT PLANNING

Edward Russell Cunningham sat on his front porch in his old paint-splattered flannel shirt, sipping an iced tea. He watched as his son and daughter drove up the long dirt road to the farmhouse. He removed his ball cap and ran a hand through his silver-gray hair. It was a ritual of his, one he had performed hundreds of times when he was an insurance agent. One last hand comb through his thick mop before the meeting. He smiled at the word.

The meeting.

Kathleen had told him that Michael and Jill had met with their advisor and that they'd been given the bad news that their retirement income wouldn't be anywhere near what they had hoped. If they wanted to have more income in their retirement years, Michael and Jill were given four options.

Edward almost laughed.

The Frustrating Four Options. As if that were all there was.

Naturally saving more money was always an option—if a person could give up something they thought they didn't need. It didn't take long for his son to stumble on the idea of terminating the whole-life insurance policies

Edward had insisted his son and daughter-in-law buy. Not so long ago Kathleen and Paul had driven up the long dirt road to propose the exact same idea.

"So, now it's Michael's turn for the talk," Edward had told his daughter on the phone last night.

"It is, Dad. I'm bringing him to the farm tomorrow."

"Well, worst case I get a few hours of free labor painting the barn."

"And best case you save Michael's retirement, like you saved mine."

They all think more money is the only answer, Edward had thought.

Edward waved as Kathleen parked her gray Honda Civic in front of the detached garage. Michael was first to step out of the car. He took a moment to glance around the family farm where he and his sister spent their childhood. It was nice to get out of the city, to come out here to the peace and quiet of the family farm. He was glad his dad had been able to hold on to it all these years.

"Michael, Kathleen, welcome." Edward gave his son and daughter a round of hugs.

In a moment, they were all on the farmhouse porch, iced teas in hand.

"So, son, your sister tells me you're here to offer free painting labor."

"Happy to help, Dad. But there is another reason I'm here." *Best to get right to it.* "Jill and I . . . "

Edward held up a hand. "Son, I know why you're here. Your sister blew your cover."

Michael was about to give Kathleen a look, but his dad kept going.

"I want you to know, Michael, that I will respect whatever you and Jill decide. It's your money, and it's your future. But if you are going to stay a few hours and help with the barn, I'd like to hear a bit more about what brought you to decide to cancel those policies."

Michael nodded. It was a reasonable request and something he planned on doing anyway. He knew those life insurance policies were important to his father, and the old man deserved to know the reasoning behind his decision.

He recounted what he had told his sister and brother-in-law the night before. The upsetting visit with their financial advisor. The bombshell news that their retirement income would be at an unacceptably low level. The disappointing options available if they wanted more out of their retirement.

"Michael and Jill had the Santa Claus meeting, Dad." Kathleen smiled.

"Everyone has it eventually," Edward nodded. "I'm guessing your advisor suggested what I call The Frustrating Four."

Michael cocked his head at his father, surprised the old man had guessed that.

"Oh, I know them all too well. They are standard solutions in the financial planning profession, son." Edward raised a finger as he presented each suggestion. "I'm guessing your advisor suggested you either save more, work longer, take on more risk, or tone down your retirement goals."

"That's exactly what he said," Michael mumbled, uncertain about whether or not he should be pleased that his father was already privy to these options.

"And so you want to cancel your whole-life insurance policies and use those premiums to put into the stock market?" Edward said.

Michael shrugged. "We need the growth. The cash value in the life insurance policies just won't grow as fast as the money in the markets."

His father rolled up his sleeve. "On that I agree, son. The markets are great for growth."

Michael waited for a moment, thinking the matter was settled. But his father merely gazed at the large lawn before them. "Tell me son, what was it that made Jill ask about retirement income at *this* meeting with your advisor in the first place?"

"Easy," Michael said. "We had a dinner party at our house the week before. Jill's father came, and he did his usual complaining about his retirement. He kept telling us he was worried about the market and worried he was going to run out of money."

"But doesn't he always worry about that?" Kathleen nudged. "What was different about that party?"

Michael looked at his sister. Indeed there *had been* something different about that party. For the first time Jill's father had brought a date, a jovial woman named Doris. Michael and Jill had instantly taken to the woman, whose warm and relaxed nature was a nice balance to Jill's father's anxiety.

Jill's father had discussed his retirement frustrations before. It's the man's favorite subject, Michael often joked. But he knew it was no joke. The man was truly terrified. He spent his retirement in constant fear, only taking out the income that he needed to survive. He didn't go on any vacations, and when Michael once inquired about this, pointing out the man clearly had the money to do so, Jill's father just barked, "I need to make my money last!"

"It's weird," Jill had once remarked. "My dad has plenty of money, but he is afraid to use it. I can't believe I am saying this, but I don't want us to be like him."

Michael and Jill had grown accustomed to Jill's father's retirement concerns. But that night's dinner party was the first time they got to hear about Doris's retirement. They had witnessed Jill's father's anxiety compared to Doris's. She had a carefree attitude about her retirement situation, and her laid-back nature struck Michael as a bit odd. She was a retired schoolteacher, and Michael assumed she couldn't have socked away anything like what Jill's parents had.

Michael relayed his thoughts to his father and sister.

"Well, I'm glad to hear old Stan has himself a girlfriend. I know it was tough on him when Lynn passed." Edward sat back in his chair. "Tell me more about the girlfriend."

"She's retired, like Jill's father. But she didn't seem to worry about money at all. She didn't worry about the markets going up and down. Unlike Jill's father, she *does* take trips. She's just more . . . present. She's happy," Michael grinned. "I hate to say this, but as much as I love Jill's father, I don't want to be like him. I want to be like his girlfriend. I mean the woman was a teacher for 25 years. She couldn't have saved anywhere near what Jill's father saved. She may have less money, but somehow she is able to do the things she wants to do. If my retirement involves being super anxious like Jill's father, then, no thank you."

"What do you think is Doris's secret?" Michael's father asked.

"That's easy," Michael said. "Being a teacher for 25 years, she has a pension. She knows exactly how much money she will receive every month, and she will receive it until the day she dies.

"One thing Doris kept saying was, 'If I live to be 110, that's my pension's problem, not mine.' That is a sharp contrast to Jill's dad, who is always saying things like, 'What if the market crashes?' or, 'What if I live to be 100?'

"Even though Doris has less money," Michael continued, "she lives like she has *more* money. I know that doesn't make sense but . . . "

Even though Doris has less money, she lives like she has *more* money.

"It makes perfect sense," Edward said.

His son had just revealed a key difference in the way people retire. Both Jill's father and Doris had done the same thing leading *up* to retirement. Jill's father had saved a portion of his income in his 401(k) plan. And Doris probably had to contribute some of her paycheck to the pension fund.

But when the time came to retire, that's when they could see the difference in their strategies.

"How," Michael asked, "could someone who has *less* money safely spend like they have more? Sure, Doris has a pension, but it's not like Jill's father is broke. The guy has a big pile of money in his retirement account."

Edward caught a slight grin on his daughter's face at the words *big pile of money*. Humored, he turned to his son.

"Let me ask you son, do you think that Doris would trade her pension for Jill's father's big pile of money?"

Michael thought for a moment. "No, I guess not."

"Isn't that an interesting observation?"

"But I still don't get why Jill's father is so worried."

"The reason Jill's father is struggling," Edward went on, "is that he has a 100 percent B.S. retirement plan."

Michael raised an eyebrow. "B.S.? You mean his plan is all . . . "

"Balance Sheet," Edward said, smiling. "Jill's father's retirement plan is 100 percent balance sheet. Millions of retirement plans focus solely on the balance sheet—growing assets as large as possible. The push is for that 'big pile of money' you mentioned."

Michael nodded. "That's what Jill and I are doing. Trying to grow the nest egg."

"A balance sheet is important, but it *alone* is not enough. The sole focus on the balance sheet has made millions of Americans ignore the single most important part of financial planning."

The sole focus on the balance sheet has made millions of Americans ignore the single most important part of financial planning.

He watched Michael pull out the small notebook his son had carried with him as long as Edward could remember. It brought a touch of joy to his heart. Not only because he had raised a boy smart enough to see the value of taking notes, but also because his son thought his words were worthy of being noted.

"Okay, Dad," Michael said. "What's the single most important part of financial planning?"

His father took a large gulp of his iced tea, leaving Michael in anticipation. He stood. "Well, that barn isn't going to get painted if we sit on the porch all day drinking iced tea. Grab those painting overalls, and let's get to it."

"On it!" Kathleen stood up and took the two pairs of overalls draped over the porch railing. She tossed a pair to her brother.

"I can give you a few hours." Michael caught the overalls as he stood up. He set them down on his chair, then clicked his pen ready to take a monsoon of notes. "But first tell me the most important part of financial planning."

"Simple." Edward descended the porch steps. "It's cash flow."

Michael's Notebook:

- Jill's father—big pile of money but is afraid to spend it. (Why?) Constantly worried about markets. (Why?)
- Doris—much smaller pile of money but has pension. Feels free to spend her pension.
- 100 percent B.S. Retirement Plan—balance sheet retirement. Important but alone not enough? (What else do you need to do?)
- Most important part of financial planning = cash flow.

CHAPTER 4

GO WITH THE FLOW

By the time Michael finished writing his thoughts, Kathleen and his father had disappeared. He put on the overalls he'd taken and jogged toward the barn and found his family inside. His sister donned overalls as well, and his father stirred a five-gallon bucket of red paint. "'Bout time you joined us."

Edward had all the supplies neatly laid out in the barn. One tall ladder, one short ladder, three buckets of paint, six brushes, and two tarps. Michael smiled at the spread. *Planning it all out,* he thought. *That's my dad.*

Michael was also grateful to learn the scraping had already been done by three college kids. All they needed to do was to paint.

"Cash flow is the whole reason you save in the first place." Edward distributed the paint into three plastic containers.

"Cash flow?" Michael buttoned the overalls. "That's *it*? Well that's what we've been doing!"

Edward covered the five-gallon bucket and glanced up at his son. "What is it you've been doing?"

Michael cocked his head and looked at his father. *Was the old man not getting it?* "Dad, Jill and I are saving up a big pile of money so we can have the retirement we want. The more money you have, the more money you can spend. It's that simple. That's the only way to do it."

Edward nodded. "It's true the more money you have, the more you can spend. But it's *not* true that's the only way to do it. Remember, it's not just about saving a big pile of money. It's about creating a plan to maximize cash flow."

It's not just about saving a big pile of money. It's about creating a plan to maximize cash flow.

Michael furrowed his brow and looked around, taking in the situation. His father, his sister, and he formed a triangle in the barn. "Dad, more money is more money. I don't see . . . " Then out of the corner of his eye, Michael caught his sister grinning. He recalled her words from last night.

What if there was a fifth option?

He smiled to himself. *They won't just tell me. I have to figure it out.*

"Okay, Dad," Michael grinned. "Lead on. We have a barn to paint."

"Kathleen, I'm going to ask you to take the tall ladder," Edward said. "I never knew my daughter would be into ninjutsu."

"It's yoga, Dad, but I don't mind. I just need help setting it up."

"Michael, you're on the shorter ladder. This old man doesn't take on any more height than he needs to."

"No problem, Dad."

* * *

Forty-five minutes later they were set up and working on the south side of the barn. Kathleen way up on the 20-foot ladder, Michael halfway up on the 10-foot ladder, and his father on the ground, swaying the paint brush back and forth.

"So, Dad," Michael said. "Tell me about cash flow."

"How about I tell you a story instead?"

Michael dipped his brush into the paint. "Okay."

His father set down his paintbrush and wiped his brow with the back of his hand. "Years ago, I had the good fortune to have dinner with a now-retired president of a multibillion-dollar insurance company. I'll call him George. We were having a friendly conversation about his company, its impeccable financial position, and how it had become the envy of so many competitors. During the conversation, I was inspired to ask what I thought was a simple question: 'George, what are you most proud of in regard to your company's current financial position?'

"Without a moment's hesitation, he replied, 'Our balance sheet of course!'

"I knew why he was so proud of it. Their balance sheet was like a beacon of light in a then-troubled economy. Their financial ratings were on the rise while others' were on the brink of being downgraded. Nonetheless, I had to disagree.

"'With all due respect,' I told him, 'I do not think your balance sheet is the most important part of your company.'"

His father picked up his paintbrush again and continued painting. "I paused for a moment, considering the enormous risk I had just taken. After all, this was the president of a multibillion-dollar company. He was not someone with whom most people disagreed, at least not verbally. George had the natural confidence that comes with being in a position of power. Finally, he looked me squarely in the eyes. Standing his ground, he reiterated his proclamation that the balance sheet was indeed the most important thing his company valued. I nodded but dared to take another chance.

"'The problem with a balance sheet,' I replied, 'is that you cannot take it into the store to buy groceries or anything else for that matter.'

"George eyed me for a few moments as an awkward silence fell upon the dinner party. Finally, the host of the party spoke up, and the conversation moved on to other matters.

"I wondered if the question had been a mistake.

"But to my surprise, the following morning I received an email from George. It read, 'Edward, our balance sheet is important, but if the answer you were looking for last night was cash flow, you are right. Cash flow matters the most.'"

His father wiped away some red paint that splattered on his arm. "It took the president of a multibillion-dollar company an entire *day* to recognize this fundamental point. Though his company had *billions* in assets, those billions didn't matter unless they could be turned into cash flow."

Edward painted with renewed vigor as he talked. "George finally came around, but *millions* of Americans will learn about the importance of cash flow too late."

Michael uttered a guttural "huh," not entirely following his father's point. "How so?"

"Think about the problem I posed to George. When was the last time you walked into the grocery store and tried to buy a gallon of milk with your retirement-account statement?"

Michael dipped his paintbrush and replied, "Never."

Kathleen called from her perch on the ladder. "But why not, Michael? Surely you have enough money in your retirement accounts to afford a gallon of milk?"

"Of course. Several thousand gallons, in fact."

"Then what's the problem?" His sister swung the brush up and down, totally comfortable so far off the ground.

"Well, we'd have to first convert the funds in our brokerage accounts into cash," he said.

"Exactly!" Edward smiled. He knew his son had just touched on a key challenge in today's retirement planning that is completely overlooked. Michael had repeated Jill's comment about her father: "It's like he had a lot of money, but he can't use it." Jill was right. Like millions of Americans, her father was standing in the grocery store aisle with a very impressive balance sheet struggling to buy a gallon of milk.

"Michael, think back to Jill's father and his girlfriend. What, in your opinion, best describes the difference between their retirements?"

"Well, like I said, Jill's father has more money, but the way he lives, it's like he has *less* income. Doris has less money but more *income*."

Edward stopped painting. "And who, in your opinion, seems happier and less stressed?"

Michael took the opportunity to stop painting as well. "Easy, Doris. With her pension, she knows exactly how much she is going to get and when."

"So, if Doris has *less* money, but *more* income, while Jill's father has *more* money but *less* income, is it fair to say that more money isn't the only solution?"

He watched his son process the question. It was the central problem with traditional retirement planning. Traditional retirement planning focused on building big piles of money, building assets. The focus is not on *income*; it's on the balance sheet. He knew that was what needed to change.

Edward set down his paintbrush and surveyed the barn. He turned to his son and took in a deep breath. Then he drew up, as he spoke the words he had spoken so many times before to so many clients. "We need to *unlearn* what we have learned about retirement planning. We need to dismantle this false concept that it's *only* about a big balance sheet—*that's* the B.S. We need to re-educate ourselves to realize that retirement planning is about positioning our assets to create safe, predictable, plentiful income."

We need to dismantle this false concept that it's *only* about a big balance sheet—*that's* the B.S.

"Safe, predictable, plentiful," Michael repeated. "Is that possible? Can we really do it?"

"Absolutely," Edward said.

"But how? I'm working as hard as I can; I don't want to cut back my retirement lifestyle; I don't want to take on any more risk; and unless I cancel that life insurance policy, I don't see where I can cut back to save an amount large enough to make a difference."

"You won't have to do any of those things, son." Edward held up his thumb. "There's a Fifth Option."

Michael looked at his father.

"A big pile of money is just bragging rights," Edward explained. "It looks impressive as you work your way *toward* retirement. But *in* retirement, what we are really concerned about is *cash flow*. That's what Doris has with her pension.

"The result of the Fifth Option is all about maximizing retirement *income*. Unlike traditional retirement planning, where saving more, working longer, risking more, or cutting back on your retirement dreams seem to be the only four answers, the Fifth Option is about strategizing your retirement plan around safe, predictable, and plentiful income."

Unlike traditional retirement planning, . . . the Fifth Option is about strategizing your retirement plan around safe, predictable, and plentiful income.

Michael dipped his paintbrush and returned to the wall in front of him. "Okay, so how do I get more income if I can't save more money?"

"There are steps you can take *now* to make certain your retirement *income* is as large as possible. The Fifth Option is not a retirement option that will happen on its own. Steps need to be taken *today*, to ensure it will work. If you don't take those steps *now*, then you are left with the Four Options, which, I think we can all agree are not pretty."

"Okay," Michael said. "So what am I supposed to do now?"

"The first thing you do is agree we will take the process one step at a time. Remember, this is about *unlearning* what has been drilled into you by the financial planning industry."

"He means he can't just tell you," Kathleen called from the ladder. "You need to get there on your own."

Michael grinned up at his sister. "Oh, wonderful. My childhood torture continues."

"Your advisor brought up several legitimate points about why your current retirement plan is not able to generate the income you want, even though it *looks* like it can."

"Sure, he did," Michael agreed. "He mentioned one challenge was that we did not know how long we were going to live. We don't know if our retirement will be three years or 30. And I know that life expectancies are on the rise. He also mentioned that past performance is no guarantee of future results. I get all that. But it's always been like that. People have always had to account for those things."

Edward picked up his paintbrush and began his smooth, gentle strokes. He knew Michael needed time to process. "Son, I cannot ask you to change your beliefs in a day. But I am going to ask you to expand your thinking. That is going to take some time."

"Well Dad, it's a big barn, so we have some time." Michael smiled. "Where does this financial transformation start?"

"The philosopher George Santayana once said, 'Those who do not study the past are condemned to repeat it.' Sadly, that's exactly where modern retirement planning has led us. We are now *condemned* to a past that we worked so hard to avoid. In short, we *deliberately* broke a system that worked quite well and returned to a system that leaves millions of people with the same fears as Jill's father. I don't want that happen to my kids."

Michael's Notebook:

- Big balance sheet (B.S.) = bragging rights
- The REAL problem is how to convert a big balance sheet into INCOME.
- Need to reeducate ourselves
- Jill's father: More *money*, less *income*
- Doris: Less *money*, more *income* (so MORE money alone isn't the answer)
- Four Options:
  - ◊ Save more
  - ◊ Work longer
  - ◊ More risk
  - ◊ Sacrifice retirement dreams
- The Fifth Option:
  - ◊ Save more *efficiently* to generate more income by strategizing your retirement plan around safe, predictable, and plentiful retirement income.

CHAPTER 5

THE THREE-LEGGED RETIREMENT STOOL

"There's an old saying," Michael's father began. "If it ain't broke, don't fix it. But sadly that's exactly what happened. We finally had a retirement model that worked, and then it all changed. Our model was dismantled and replaced with something not nearly as effective. Society, for the most part, has not adapted, even though the environment is different. Now we are starting to see the consequences with today's retirement planning. And as you learned from your recent visit with your advisor, the consequences of what we did are dire."

"How so?" Michael moved his ladder further down the barn wall.

"Today, for most people, most of the responsibility for funding retirement is up to them. That is exactly how it was just a few generations ago.

Today, for most people, most of the responsibility for funding retirement is up to them. That is exactly how it was just a few generations ago.

"It seems almost unbelievable, but just a few generations ago, the concept of retirement simply did not exist for most people. Back then, there was little need to think about retirement. The average life expectancy in the early 1800s was only 37 years. So most people just worked their whole lives.[1]

"Even in the early 1900s, the situation was still the same. When a worker could no longer physically work, they were taken in by their children, and they cared for grandchildren or they helped with household chores. Someone less fortunate or without family often became a ward of the state. But the majority of people simply continued to work until they died."[2]

"Sounds a bit grim," Michael said.

"It was," his father agreed. "But remember, the workplace was also different. It wasn't until late in the 19th century that society unknowingly began setting the stage for the building blocks of the three-legged retirement stool," Edward said. "And with it the notion of retirement was born."

"Three-legged what?"

Edward moved over to an unpainted section of the barn. He picked up a brush and drew a simple three-legged stool on the wall. He wrote the word *retirement* on the seat of the stool and wrote the word *pension* on one of the legs.

"Picture your retirement as a three-legged stool that will support you in your golden years. The first leg was the pension. In 1875, American Express, which had started as a freight company a couple of decades earlier, implemented the first recorded pension in US history.[3]

"Ironically, that company's pension idea was rooted in the notion that a pension could benefit *both* the corporation and its employees. The goal was to provide an incentive for employees to remain with the company. But it also created a gentle way to get rid of aging workers. At the time, life expectancies were still comparatively short, so American Express knew it would not be on the hook to pay retirees for long.[4]

"Soon other companies, specifically railroad and shipping companies, followed suit. It was to their advantage to keep workers who had some valued knowledge or skill. Those workers needed to be retained. And to some degree, a pension did provide a humane way for older workers to leave the workforce to make room for new blood.

"Pensions allowed employees to focus on their jobs. They had peace of mind knowing that they could actually stop working because they had a guaranteed income for the rest of their lives.

"Pensions fostered a sense of appreciation between employees and employers. A sense of loyalty emerged because a social contract had been made."

"So American Express was the first pension?" Michael asked.

"Actually," Kathleen jumped in, "the idea of pensions can be traced all the way back to the Roman Empire. The Romans offered pensions to soldiers after they completed their military service. Since then many nations have offered pensions to those who served in their military, sort of like a thank you to their soldiers. But Rome didn't really want a bunch of trained retired soldiers with no income because such men would make easy targets to recruit for an uprising. So the government quelled that possibility by paying pensions.[5]

"While the concept of pensions goes back thousands of years, what is significant about the American Express pension is that it was the first pension offered by a *private* company in the United States," Kathleen said. "It opened the door for more to come, and come they did. Slowly, more companies jumped into the pension game, and in 1913 pensions got a big push."

"Why?" Michael asked.

"Congress passed the first federal income tax." Kathleen, who had finished with every possible spot she could reach, descended the ladder.

"Ahh," Michael smiled. "Doomsday."

"The first income tax meant a lot of changes for a lot of people," Edward jumped in. "But it also allowed corporations to *deduct* pensions paid to retired employees as a business expense. Companies now had a financial incentive to offer them. This opened the door to what could be regarded as the Golden Age of Pensions.[6]

"Over the next 20 years, more than 300 pension plans were introduced, covering 15 percent of the nation's workers. By the late 1990s, pension plans were offered by more than 45 percent of companies in the United States.[7]

"Millions of workers would share the dream that there was life after work," Edward went on. "They could now look forward to a guaranteed income that would support them."

"That makes sense," Michael said. "Doris mentioned she and her late husband never talked about retirement planning. They worked to pay off their mortgage, and their pensions took care of the rest."

"With so many people covered under a pension," Edward said, "and with life expectancies much shorter than they are today, there wasn't the need for the kind of planning we have to do nowadays."

"But the pension is just one leg, right?" Michael said.

"That's right," Edward said. "Can you guess what the second leg is?"

"Social Security?" Michael said.

"Correct. While 1913 was a pivotal year for pensions, 1935 was the year of Social Security. Motivated by the Great Depression, President Franklin D. Roosevelt signed the Social Security Act into law. The idea was to provide ongoing income assistance for retired workers age 65 and older.

"Originally, Social Security was a safety net for people who lived longer than expected. It provided another source of income. The initial purpose for Social Security was really longevity insurance. Most folks were not expected to even make it to 65."[8]

"Those who did, only drew on it for a few short years," Kathleen explained as she moved the ladder with the help of her father.

"That's quite a departure from today," Michael said. "Probably not what Roosevelt had in mind when he proposed the idea."

Kathleen grabbed the ladder and prepared to climb. "Interestingly, Roosevelt wasn't the first person to propose this idea."

"Really?" Michael looked at his sister. "A previous president suggested it?"

"Not a president, a *chancellor*," Kathleen said. "In the late 1800s, Otto von Bismarck was the chancellor of Germany. He was many things, including a master politician. In order to win political favor, Bismarck established a program to pay a disability payment to people after they could no longer work."[9]

"Back then, people thought anyone over age 65 was no longer mentally capable."

"Seriously?" Michael chuckled.

"Different times, son," Edward said. "Different times."

"Chancellor Bismarck created what could be considered the world's first social security plan. Unlike other government pensions that only went to military members or government workers, Bismarck's plan was for everyone. He paved the way for Roosevelt to propose a similar plan that included everybody."

"But Social Security has some issues," Michael said.

"It does. The ratio of people receiving income and people contributing has narrowed. Some changes need to be made, or one day the system will not be able to fund itself."

"But for the moment, we still have only two legs of the three-legged retirement stool."

"Correct." Edward painted the words *Social Security* on the second leg. "Now let's look at the final of the three legs. Leg Three is your own personal savings, like retirement accounts, real estate, and bank accounts." Edward painted the words *personal savings* on the third leg.

"A generation ago, people didn't lean on the third leg as much as they do today. The majority of their retirement needs were *guaranteed*. Social Security and pensions took care of most of what people required. All they needed to do was be sure they paid off their mortgage, which most people did.

"In short, retirement flourished, because life expectancies were on the rise, creating the *time* to retire, and those rising life expectancies were funded by *guaranteed* income streams."

"That sounds like Doris," Michael said. "She didn't save a lot, because she never earned a lot. But her pension sure allows her to *do* a lot. She's not fearful of outliving her money."

"Unfortunately, that's the opposite of Jill's father." Michael dipped his paintbrush, then paused. "I still don't see what the problem is, though. He has a lot of money. He's averaging a good return."

"That's true," Edward said. "If Jill's father had a pension, he might be more confident in his retirement. But he doesn't have one. In other words, he *doesn't* have a way to turn his money into safe, predictable, plentiful income. In the past, pensions did that for us. Now with pensions drying up, we're on our own. Jill's father is the poster boy for the problem we created.

"The most important leg of the three-legged stool has been whittled away right underneath us. The pension, which millions of people counted on for their financial safety, has all but disappeared.

> # The pension, which millions of people counted on for their financial safety, has all but disappeared.

"This is why people are so concerned about retirement planning. Over the last 30 years, corporate America has been shifting the risk of retirement planning back to the individual. As pension doors began to close, Wall Street stepped in and opened new ones. There were choices, *thousands* of choices. Mutual funds, index funds, hybrid funds, reverse mortgages. We as a society became mesmerized by the abundance of choices." Edward sighed, thinking back to simpler times.

"When did pensions start to disappear?" Michael asked.

"The trend started in the late 1970s, when Congress passed a small, but soon to be historic piece of legislation that would go on to change the financial planning industry forever," Edward said. "This piece of legislation gave companies an option to replace their pensions. And it all started with a man named Ted Benna."[10]

Michael furrowed his brow. He had never heard of Ted Benna. He looked up at his sister.

Kathleen smiled down at him. "Ted Benna is known as the Father of the 401(k)," she said. "Benna was a human resources consultant, and he was always looking for ways to better serve the companies that were his clients. When Congress passed the Revenue Act of 1978, Benna took a close look at the passage that was Section 401(k).

"That section established qualified deferred compensation plans, which allowed people to save money with pretax dollars. Originally, they were known as income-reduction plans.

"Few people realize that the addition of this code was designed as a *minor* change to allow the few highly paid workers in a company to have an additional option for retirement. It was never meant to catch on the way it did. It was never meant to be *the* retirement option; it was merely meant to be a supplement.

"What Benna figured out was that the 401(k) could be utilized by *anyone* at a company, not just the highest earners. His discovery paved the way for companies to completely change the retirement benefits they offered to employees.

"Ironically, the ability for wealthy workers to save additional funds would contribute to the undoing of the three-legged stool and impact all workers. The coveted first leg, the pension, disappeared."

"Now that the 401(k) existed, companies could divert the money that would have gone to the pension to other areas. A pension was an expense that could now be skillfully eliminated. Operations could now offload the burden of retirement planning and risk to their employees.

"And offload they did. In 1998, 60 percent of Fortune 500 companies provided pension plans to new hires. By the end of 2013, that number had fallen to only 24 percent. Today, while many government jobs still offer pensions, less than 20 percent of the private sector workforce has access to a pension, and that number is in decline.[11]

"The saddest part," Edward sighed, "can be seen in the difference between people who are saving for retirement and the people who are already retired. People saving for their retirement still *believe* they can make it work. Even though they are on their own, they still believe they can save enough money to have a comfortable retirement. They still believe that *somehow* it will all work out."

Edward pointed to the third leg on the image of the stool. "This may be the most dangerous part of the B.S.-only retirement plan. It *looks* like it will work. We all look at our big brokerage statements and say, 'Yep, I'm on track. I may not have a pension, but I have a big pile of money, and it will all work out.'

"The trouble is, that's total B.S." Edward smiled at his son, "Retirement income doesn't work the way people think it does, and they will realize that too late."

Retirement income doesn't work the way people think it does, and they will realize that too late.

Michael set down his paintbrush and shook his head. "Sorry, but I don't follow. I understand that a pension is guaranteed income, so it's easier to plan. But why can't Jill's father just take out more money? As long as he takes out less than his average rate of return, he should be fine."

Edward shook his head. "I know it looks that way. And I'll be the first to admit, Jill's father might be fine. In fact, he might do extremely well. But the problem is he can't *know* for sure. And the reason he can't know for sure is because of the Desert Island Problem."

Michael furrowed his brow. "What's the Desert Island Problem?"

Michael's Notebook:

- For centuries the concept of retirement didn't exist. Most people worked until they died.
- Pension time line:
  - ◊ Roman Empire—offered pensions to retired soldiers
  - ◊ Late 1800s—American Express created the first private pension in the United States
  - ◊ Late 1800s (Germany)—Otto von Bismarck offered first social security plan
  - ◊ 1913—first federal income tax (pension contributions now deductible)
  - ◊ 1935—Social Security Act passed
  - ◊ 1913–1970s—Golden Age of Pensions
  - ◊ Late 1970s—Section 401(k) introduced (pensions began to decline)
  - ◊ Ted Benna = Father of the 401(k)
  - ◊ Today—pensions are rare; Social Security does not cover basic living expenses; responsibility 100 percent on us
- Three-legged retirement stool:
  - ◊ Pensions (rare)
  - ◊ Social Security (uncertain)
  - ◊ Personal savings (IRA, 401[k], bank accounts)—this is what most people rely on to get them through retirement. Is it enough?
- Desert Island Problem???

CHAPTER 6

THE DESERT ISLAND PROBLEM

"The Desert Island Problem is the reason your retirement income *has* to be low," Edward said. "In the past, when most people had pensions, a lot of the retirement work was done *for* retirees. Today," he let out a long breath, "well, today people are on their own. And, as I mentioned, their retirement doesn't work the way they think it does."

Michael nodded. "Dad, I get that pensions are by and large gone. And I get that people are on their own. But Jill's father is just being overly cautious. He doesn't understand the markets the way I do. If you can earn a decent average return, as long as you take out *less* than that return, you'll be fine. So I think we can take out more money than our advisor is telling us. Jill and I are not going to have the same fears as her father."

"You say that now, but when you get to retirement your attitudes will change. Let me prove it to you."

Michael had never seen the old man so serious.

Edward quickly caught the tension and smiled. "I need to tell you a story. But it's too important to be distracted by this barn. Let's all take a break. I'll ask my ninja daughter to come down off the ladder. Michael, in the barn fridge, there is a pitcher of iced tea and three glasses. We'll meet you under the chestnut tree. There, I'll prove to you why your advisor is right."

Michael had to admit he was intrigued. He set down his paintbrush and hopped off his ladder. He clumsily grabbed the pitcher of iced tea and three chilled glasses from the fridge and headed out to meet his father and sister under the old chestnut tree on the front lawn.

After the iced tea was poured, Edward spoke. "Imagine you are shipwrecked and stranded on a desert island. The island provides all the food you need with fish and fruit trees. But you were only able to save one barrel of water from the ship. So you have plenty of food," Edward held up a finger, "but only *one* barrel of water. The question is, how much water do you drink every day?"

Michael paused before answering, sensing one of his old man's teaching moments. "Well, that would depend on how often it rains and on how long it was before I was rescued."

"And being stranded alone on the island, would you know the answer to either of those questions?"

"No," Michael said quickly.

"So I ask again," Edward grinned, "how much water would you drink every day?"

Again Michael paused, trying to see where his father was headed. But logic dictated the answer. "That's simple, Dad. I would drink the absolute minimum amount of water a human being would need to survive."

"Okay. Now let's suppose you were able to save *two* barrels from your ship. Now you have two barrels. How much water would you drink every day?"

"I have to admit, I *still* would drink the minimum amount I needed to survive."

"Bingo! That is *exactly* what your advisor was trying to tell you. Modern retirement planning has become all about *survival*. You *must* make your money last. You have no choice." Edward reached over and gently touched his son's arm. "This is why Jill's father is so anxious about his money. He has a big barrel of water, but he has to take small sips because he has no idea when the barrel will fill up again, and he has no idea how long he needs to make the water last. In short, his retirement consists of two things: stressing and guessing."

You *must* make your money last. You have no choice.

"Stressing and guessing," Michael repeated. "I like that."

"It does have a nice ring to it," Edward smiled. "But it really is how most people go through retirement."

Kathleen nudged Michael's arm. "Time to pull out that notebook of yours."

"On our hypothetical desert island," Edward continued, "we are constantly doing two things: stressing and guessing."

Michael thumbed open his notebook. He smiled as wrote the words *stressing* and *guessing* on a clean page.

"We are guessing when we will be rescued, and we are stressing about when it is going to rain. Those are the two risks that are forever on the mind of the desert island castaway. In the retirement world, we have the same two problems. We do not know how long we are going to live, and we do not know how the market will perform.

"If we knew the *exact* day we were going to die, then we could determine how much we could spend. But we don't know if our retirement will be three years or 30. If it were three years, we could spend quite lavishly. But if it were 30 years, we'd be a lot more frugal. Since we don't know, everyone is forced to take small sips."

"We're stressing and guessing," Michael said.

"Exactly, son. We are *guessing* how long we are going to live, and we are *stressing* about the ups and downs of the markets. The uncertainty of how long we are going to live is referred to as *longevity risk*. And the uncertainty of the markets is referred to as *volatility risk*."

We are *guessing* how long we are going to live, and we are *stressing* about the ups and downs of the markets.

Michael scratched the words in his notebook:

Longevity risk—the uncertainty of how long a retiree is going to live.

Volatility risk—the uncertainty of how the markets will perform.

Edward tapped the open page of the notebook. "Those two risks right there—longevity risk and volatility risk—are the reasons a person's retirement doesn't work the way they think it does. During their working years, they don't realize that no matter how much money they save, they will have to take small sips. The consequence of running out of money is so unthinkable that we all have to live with lower incomes than we anticipated."

Those two risks right there—longevity risk and volatility risk—are the reasons a person's retirement doesn't work the way they think it does.

Edward drank his iced tea. "The retirement you dreamed of might not come true. Being on the desert island, the *worst* thing you could do is drink water during an extended period of no rain. But the trouble is, you *have* to drink something. So, you drink the smallest amount. Maybe the next day it rains and fills your barrel back up. Or maybe it's dry for three weeks. You just don't know, so you are ultra-cautious.

"The same thing is true with retirement. You said it yourself, 'It's like Jill's father has a lot of money, but he is afraid to spend it.' That's exactly right. He's on his retirement desert island. He has this big barrel of water, but he has to take small sips.

"Are you starting to see the challenge that Jill's father has? He has a big barrel of money. But it is not *accessible*. He cannot withdraw from it in an efficient way that will ensure it will last. That's why he is forced to withdraw such a low amount. His girlfriend, on the other hand, doesn't have to play that game. She has a smaller barrel, but her barrel continually gets *refilled*. That's why she doesn't worry. To her, the desert island is a vacation!"

Michael smiled as he wrote. He could see the two major challenges with retirement planning. Once a person retired, they had no idea how long they were going to live. And the markets could have large swings in any one year.

Then an idea occurred to him.

"Okay, I understand the risks of longevity and volatility. And I understand the comparison of a big barrel of water on a desert island."

Michael set down his notebook. "However, Jill's father's retirement account, just like my retirement account, *averages* a rate of return. So, over time, his money *grows*. As long as he does not withdraw more than his average rate of return, he should be fine. If he's averaging say, 9 percent per year, he could take out 8 percent. Or even 7 percent to be safe. There's no need to go any lower than that."

Kathleen cleared her throat. "That, baby brother, is the single most dangerous belief in all of financial planning."

Michael's Notebook:

- Modern retirement planning = stressing and guessing
- Desert Island Problem: You are on a desert island with plenty of food but only one barrel of water. How much water do you drink every day? Big barrel, small sips.
  ◊ You drink the smallest amount possible because:
    — You don't know when you will be rescued (longevity risk).
    — You don't know when it will rain again (volatility risk).
- The two Desert Island questions:
  ◊ How long are you going to live (longevity risk)?
  ◊ What returns are you going to get (volatility risk)?
- But my retirement account *grows*. As long as I withdraw *less* than my average rate of return, I should be fine.
  ◊ Sis says that's the most dangerous belief in **all** of financial planning.
  ◊ MOST DANGEROUS??? WHY???

CHAPTER 7

THE MOST DANGEROUS BELIEF

I *f I am earning an average of 8 percent on my retirement portfolio, why can't I just withdraw 7 percent each year? Or even 6 percent?* Michael reran the idea and his sister's comment in his head, before blurting, "How is withdrawing less than your average rate of return the most dangerous . . . "

"I know," his father cut in. "It seems like hyperbole. But your sister is right. That line of thinking *is* the most dangerous belief a person could have about their retirement plan."

"But how?" Michael insisted.

Edward took another drink. "Tell you what. The barn isn't going to paint itself. Let's plow through till lunch, and then I'll explain."

Michael nodded, still wondering what could possibly be wrong with a retiree withdrawing *less* than they earn.

* * *

By noon the entire south wall of the barn was completely covered with a deep red. His father stepped back to admire their work. "Now that's a thing of beauty. Michael, Kathleen, come on down. You both earned a good meal."

After they had cleaned up, Michael and Kathleen found a plate of sandwiches, a big green salad, and a bowl of potato chips on the picnic table. Another cold pitcher of iced tea awaited them.

"Wow, Dad." Michael sat. "I never knew you were such a host."

"You have to feed your workers." Edward took a seat and propped a brown leather briefcase on the bench next to him. "We're talking about not running out of money during your retirement. With the right planning, anyone can leave something behind to their kids."

"With all due respect, Dad, I feel like Jill and I *have* been doing the right planning. I'm still stuck on this idea that if I earn an average of 8 percent per year in my retirement investments, why can't I withdraw 7 percent? I don't see the problem."

Edward passed plates to his children. "Let's take a real-world example. Let's see how easy it is to get a false sense of hope with B.S.-only retirement planning."

"Okaaaayy." Michael detected the sarcasm in his father's voice.

"Suppose your portfolio earned an average return of 11.90 percent. Would you feel comfortable withdrawing 10 percent each year?"

"Absolutely. If I am averaging 11.90 percent and I'm only taking out 10 percent, that's a 1.90 percent cushion to protect me."

"You're right." Edward handed his son a sheet of paper with a 25-year sample retirement chart. The retiree began with $1 million in their portfolio and withdrew $100,000, or 10 percent, of that number every year. Even though the market had its ups and downs, the retiree's portfolio had *averaged* 11.90 percent per year. Just as Michael predicted, the retiree's retirement strategy worked out just fine. There was more than $1.9 *million* in the account at the time of the retiree's death.

Michael put his finger on the $1,937,911.23 number at the bottom of the chart. "There it is Dad, right in plain sight. As long as you take out less than what you average, you'll do fine. $1.9 million left over. That's a nice legacy for the kids."

Will your million dollars last if you average 11.90%?[1]

Retirement Year	Actual Year	Beginning Year Balance	Withdrawal	Post Withdrawal Balance	S&P Return	End of Year Balance
1	1995	$1,000,000.00	$100,000.00	$900,000.00	38.02%	$1,242,180.00
2	1996	$1,242,180.00	$100,000.00	$1,142,180.00	23.06%	$1,405,566.71
3	1997	$1,405,566.71	$100,000.00	$1,305,566.71	33.67%	$1,745,151.02
4	1998	$1,745,151.02	$100,000.00	$1,645,151.02	28.73%	$2,117,802.91
5	1999	$2,117,802.91	$100,000.00	$2,017,802.91	21.11%	$2,443,761.10
6	2000	$2,443,761.10	$100,000.00	$2,343,761.10	-9.11%	$2,130,244.46
7	2001	$2,130,244.46	$100,000.00	$2,030,244.46	-11.98%	$1,787,021.18
8	2002	$1,787,021.18	$100,000.00	$1,687,021.18	-22.27%	$1,311,321.56
9	2003	$1,311,321.56	$100,000.00	$1,211,321.56	28.72%	$1,559,213.11
10	2004	$1,559,213.11	$100,000.00	$1,459,213.11	10.82%	$1,617,099.97
11	2005	$1,617,099.97	$100,000.00	$1,517,099.97	4.79%	$1,589,769.06
12	2006	$1,589,769.06	$100,000.00	$1,489,769.06	15.74%	$1,724,258.71
13	2007	$1,724,258.71	$100,000.00	$1,624,258.71	5.46%	$1,712,943.24
14	2008	$1,712,943.24	$100,000.00	$1,612,943.24	-37.22%	$1,012,605.76
15	2009	$1,012,605.76	$100,000.00	$912,605.76	27.11%	$1,160,013.19
16	2010	$1,160,013.19	$100,000.00	$1,060,013.19	14.87%	$1,217,637.15
17	2011	$1,217,637.15	$100,000.00	$1,117,637.15	2.07%	$1,140,772.24
18	2012	$1,140,772.24	$100,000.00	$1,040,772.24	15.88%	$1,206,046.87
19	2013	$1,206,046.87	$100,000.00	$1,106,046.87	32.43%	$1,464,737.87
20	2014	$1,464,737.87	$100,000.00	$1,364,737.87	13.81%	$1,553,208.17
21	2015	$1,553,208.17	$100,000.00	$1,453,208.17	1.31%	$1,472,245.19
22	2016	$1,472,245.19	$100,000.00	$1,372,245.19	11.93%	$1,535,954.04
23	2017	$1,535,954.04	$100,000.00	$1,435,954.04	21.94%	$1,751,002.36
24	2018	$1,751,002.36	$100,000.00	$1,651,002.36	-4.41%	$1,578,193.16
25	2019	$1,578,193.16	$100,000.00	$1,478,193.16	31.10%	$1,937,911.23
				Average Rate of Return	11.90%	

Figure 7.1

"You're right. This person's financial advisor can clap her hands together and say, 'My work here is done!' You see how easy it can be?" His father smiled.

Then Michael caught his sister smiling. He knew something was up. "It seems a bit too easy."

Edward brightened. "Agreed. The danger is actually staring you right in the face, but you can't see it."

Michael stared at the chart, trying to figure out what was wrong. "Well, an 11.90 percent average return might be a little high. I'm not sure the market averaged that. But yeah, that's the idea. Withdraw less than you earn, and you'll be fine."

His sister continued grinning. "Would you say that you are even *safer* with a higher average return? For example, if this retiree averaged, say 13.68 percent, but still took out just 10 percent, then he should have even *more* money, right? The bigger the gap, the bigger the bucks?"

Michael studied the grin, knowing something was up. But the math was there. "Yes, if two retirees are both withdrawing 10 percent, the retiree with the higher average rate of return will have more money."

"Can't argue with that, can we, Dad?" Kathleen smiled at her father.

"Okay, what's up?" Michael said. "What's wrong with that logic?"

Edward removed another sheet and slid it in front of Michael. He looked down at the chart and his mouth fell open.

"Wait . . . how . . . ?"

Michael saw that the chart spanned a 30-year retirement. Like the previous example, this retiree began with $1 million and withdrew $100,000, or 10 percent of that number, per year. The average rate of return for the 30-year period was 13.68 percent, a full 3.68 percent *higher* than the percentage they were withdrawing. But despite having a *higher* average rate of return, this retiree ran out of money in the 13th year.

Michael shook his head. "I don't . . . I don't get it."

"Let me ask you, son," Edward said, "does the market earn the same return each and every year?"

"Of course not." Michael pointed to the chart. "They're different every year."

"Exactly. The market yields *different* returns *each* year. Sometimes the returns are negative. Sometimes *very* negative. If the market did return the same percentages each year, then retirement planning would be easy, and no one would ever be worried. The numbers would work out perfectly, just like you described."

Will your milion dollars last if you average 13.68%?

Retirement Year	Actual Year	Beginning Year Balance	Withdrawal	Post Withdrawal Balance	S&P Return	End of Year Balance
1	1972	$1,000,000.00	$100,000.00	$900,000.00	19.15%	$1,072,350.00
2	1973	$1,072,350.00	$100,000.00	$972,350.00	-15.03%	$826,205.80
3	1974	$826,205.80	$100,000.00	$726,205.80	-26.95%	$530,493.33
4	1975	$530,493.33	$100,000.00	$430,493.33	38.46%	$596,061.07
5	1976	$596,061.07	$100,000.00	$496,061.07	24.20%	$616,107.85
6	1977	$616,107.85	$100,000.00	$516,107.85	-7.78%	$475,954.66
7	1978	$475,954.66	$100,000.00	$375,954.66	6.41%	$400,053.35
8	1979	$400,053.35	$100,000.00	$300,053.35	18.69%	$356,133.32
9	1980	$356,133.32	$100,000.00	$256,133.32	32.67%	$339,812.08
10	1981	$339,812.08	$100,000.00	$239,812.08	-5.33%	$227,030.09
11	1982	$227,030.09	$100,000.00	$127,030.09	21.22%	$153,985.88
12	1983	$153,985.88	$100,000.00	$53,985.88	23.13%	$66,472.82
13	1984	$66,472.82	$100,000.00	$0	5.96%	$0
14	1985	$0	$100,000.00	$0	32.24%	$0
15	1986	$0	$100,000.00	$0	19.06%	$0
16	1987	$0	$100,000.00	$0	5.69%	$0
17	1988	$0	$100,000.00	$0	16.64%	$0
18	1989	$0	$100,000.00	$0	32.00%	$0
19	1990	$0	$100,000.00	$0	-3.42%	$0
20	1991	$0	$100,000.00	$0	30.95%	$0
21	1992	$0	$100,000.00	$0	7.60%	$0
22	1993	$0	$100,000.00	$0	10.17%	$0
23	1994	$0	$100,000.00	$0	1.19%	$0
24	1995	$0	$100,000.00	$0	38.02%	$0
25	1996	$0	$100,000.00	$0	23.06%	$0
26	1997	$0	$100,000.00	$0	33.67%	$0
27	1998	$0	$100,000.00	$0	28.73%	$0
28	1999	$0	$100,000.00	$0	21.11%	$0
29	2000	$0	$100,000.00	$0	-9.11%	$0
30	2001	$0	$100,000.00	$0	-11.98%	$0
			Average Rate of Return		13.68%	

At this point, the retiree is out of money. They cannot make another $100,000 withdrawal.

Figure 7.2

Edward tapped the chart. "The problem is that even though the market 'averaged' 13.68 percent per year, it had a *variation* of returns to make up that average."

He slid another chart on the table.

What is the average return of the S&P from 1972–2001?

Actual Year	S&P Return
1972	19.15%
1973	-15.03%
1974	-26.95%
1975	38.46%
1976	24.20%
1977	-7.78%
1978	6.41%
1979	18.69%
1980	32.67%
1981	-5.33%
1982	21.22%
1983	23.13%
1984	5.96%
1985	32.24%
1986	19.06%
1987	5.69%
1988	16.64%
1989	32.00%
1990	-3.42%
1991	30.95%
1992	7.60%
1993	10.17%
1994	1.19%
1995	38.02%
1996	23.06%
1997	33.67%
1998	28.73%
1999	21.11%
2000	-9.11%
2001	-11.98%
Average Rate of Return	**13.68%**

Figure 7.3

"From 1972 to 2001 the market *did* average 13.68 percent per year. As you can see, some years the returns were quite good, while in other years, the returns were negative. But overall, it was a very good time to retire."

"The funny thing," Kathleen jumped in, "is that in our list of actual returns, there is not *one* year where we actually earned 13.68 percent. It just happens to be our *average* rate of return."

Edward slid another sheet of paper across the table but kept it face down. "Let me ask you something, son. If I take those returns and reverse them, will I still get the same average?"

"Of course. You can take all 30 of those numbers and scramble them up any way you like. If you add them together and divide by 30, you will *always* get 13.68 percent."

"That's right. That is *exactly* how it works." Edward flipped the piece of paper over. It revealed the same years but reversed, beginning with 2001 and ending with 1972. Michael saw that even though the years were reversed, the average rate of return was still 13.68 percent.

Is the average return the same if
we reverse the years to 2001–1972?

Actual Year	S&P Return
2001	-11.98%
2000	-9.11%
1999	21.11%
1998	28.73%
1997	33.67%
1996	23.06%
1995	38.02%
1994	1.19%
1993	10.17%
1992	7.60%
1991	30.95%
1990	-3.42%
1989	32.00%
1988	16.64%
1987	5.69%
1986	19.06%
1985	32.24%
1984	5.96%
1983	23.13%
1982	21.22%
1981	-5.33%
1980	32.67%
1979	18.69%
1978	6.41%
1977	-7.78%
1976	24.20%
1975	38.46%
1974	-26.95%
1973	-15.03%
1972	19.15%
Average Rate of Return	**13.68%**

Figure 7.4

"We can scramble the years any way we like, and the *average* will *always* be the same," Edward said. "But when it comes to *money*, the results are drastically different." He pointed to the chart of the retiree who retired in 1972. "Let's call this retiree Sam. We know Sam ran out of money in 1984, the 13th year of his retirement."

Will your million dollars last if you average 13.68%?

Retirement Year	Actual Year	Beginning Year Balance	Withdrawal	Post Withdrawal Balance	S&P Return	End of Year Balance
1	1972	$1,000,000.00	$100,000.00	$900,000.00	19.15%	$1,072,350.00
2	1973	$1,072,350.00	$100,000.00	$972,350.00	-15.03%	$826,205.80
3	1974	$826,205.80	$100,000.00	$726,205.80	-26.95%	$530,493.33
4	1975	$530,493.33	$100,000.00	$430,493.33	38.46%	$596,061.07
5	1976	$596,061.07	$100,000.00	$496,061.07	24.20%	$616,107.85
6	1977	$616,107.85	$100,000.00	$516,107.85	-7.78%	$475,954.66
7	1978	$475,954.66	$100,000.00	$375,954.66	6.41%	$400,053.35
8	1979	$400,053.35	$100,000.00	$300,053.35	18.69%	$356,133.32
9	1980	$356,133.32	$100,000.00	$256,133.32	32.67%	$339,812.08
10	1981	$339,812.08	$100,000.00	$239,812.08	-5.33%	$227,030.09
11	1982	$227,030.09	$100,000.00	$127,030.09	21.22%	$153,985.88
12	1983	$153,985.88	$100,000.00	$53,985.88	23.13%	$66,472.82
13	1984	$66,472.82	$100,000.00	$0	5.96%	$0
14	1985	$0	$100,000.00	$0	32.24%	$0
15	1986	$0	$100,000.00	$0	19.06%	$0
16	1987	$0	$100,000.00	$0	5.69%	$0
17	1988	$0	$100,000.00	$0	16.64%	$0
18	1989	$0	$100,000.00	$0	32.00%	$0
19	1990	$0	$100,000.00	$0	-3.42%	$0
20	1991	$0	$100,000.00	$0	30.95%	$0
21	1992	$0	$100,000.00	$0	7.60%	$0
22	1993	$0	$100,000.00	$0	10.17%	$0
23	1994	$0	$100,000.00	$0	1.19%	$0
24	1995	$0	$100,000.00	$0	38.02%	$0
25	1996	$0	$100,000.00	$0	23.06%	$0
26	1997	$0	$100,000.00	$0	33.67%	$0
27	1998	$0	$100,000.00	$0	28.73%	$0
28	1999	$0	$100,000.00	$0	21.11%	$0
29	2000	$0	$100,000.00	$0	-9.11%	$0
30	2001	$0	$100,000.00	$0	-11.98%	$0
			Average Rate of Return		13.68%	

At this point, the retiree is out of money. They cannot make another $100,000 withdrawal.

Figure 7.5

"Amazing," Michael said.

"What's *really* amazing, son, is when I *reverse* those years. Here is a chart of those same years in reverse, beginning in 2001 and ending in 1972. In this scenario, *you have a very pleased retiree.*"

In this scenario, your million dollars averaged 13.68% and it did last

Retirement Year	Actual Year	Beginning Year Balance	Withdrawal	Post Withdrawal Balance	S&P Return	End of Year Balance
1	2001	$1,000,000.00	$100,000.00	$900,000.00	-11.98%	$792,180.00
2	2000	$792,180.00	$100,000.00	$692,180.00	-9.11%	$629,122.40
3	1999	$629,122.40	$100,000.00	$529,122.40	21.11%	$640,820.14
4	1998	$640,820.14	$100,000.00	$540,820.14	28.73%	$696,197.77
5	1997	$696,197.77	$100,000.00	$596,197.77	33.67%	$796,937.56
6	1996	$796,937.56	$100,000.00	$696,937.56	23.06%	$857,651.36
7	1995	$857,651.36	$100,000.00	$757,651.36	38.02%	$1,045,710.40
8	1994	$1,045,710.40	$100,000.00	$945,710.40	1.19%	$956,964.36
9	1993	$956,964.36	$100,000.00	$856,964.36	10.17%	$944,117.63
10	1992	$944,117.63	$100,000.00	$844,117.63	7.60%	$908,270.57
11	1991	$908,270.57	$100,000.00	$808,270.57	30.95%	$1,058,430.31
12	1990	$1,058,430.31	$100,000.00	$958,430.31	-3.42%	$925,652.00
13	1989	$925,652.00	$100,000.00	$825,652.00	32.00%	$1,089,860.63
14	1988	$1,089,860.63	$100,000.00	$989,860.63	16.64%	$1,154,573.44
15	1987	$1,154,573.44	$100,000.00	$1,054,573.44	5.69%	$1,114,578.67
16	1986	$1,114,578.67	$100,000.00	$1,014,578.67	19.06%	$1,207,957.37
17	1985	$1,207,957.37	$100,000.00	$1,107,957.37	32.24%	$1,465,162.82
18	1984	$1,465,162.82	$100,000.00	$1,365,162.82	5.96%	$1,446,526.53
19	1983	$1,446,526.53	$100,000.00	$1,346,526.53	23.13%	$1,657,978.11
20	1982	$1,657,978.11	$100,000.00	$1,557,978.11	21.22%	$1,888,581.07
21	1981	$1,888,581.07	$100,000.00	$1,788,581.07	-5.33%	$1,693,249.70
22	1980	$1,693,249.70	$100,000.00	$1,593,249.70	32.67%	$2,113,764.37
23	1979	$2,113,764.37	$100,000.00	$2,013,764.37	18.69%	$2,390,136.94
24	1978	$2,390,136.94	$100,000.00	$2,290,136.94	6.41%	$2,436,934.71
25	1977	$2,436,934.71	$100,000.00	$2,336,934.71	-7.78%	$2,155,121.19
26	1976	$2,155,121.19	$100,000.00	$2,055,121.19	24.20%	$2,552,460.52
27	1975	$2,552,460.52	$100,000.00	$2,452,460.52	38.46%	$3,395,676.84
28	1974	$3,395,676.84	$100,000.00	$3,295,676.84	-26.95%	$2,407,491.93
29	1973	$2,407,491.93	$100,000.00	$2,307,491.93	-15.03%	$1,960,675.89
30	1972	$1,960,675.89	$100,000.00	$1,860,675.89	19.15%	$2,216,995.33
				Average Rate of Return	13.68%	

Figure 7.6

Michael shook his head as he looked at the chart. Simply by reversing the years, *this* retiree, with the *same* amount of starting money and the *same* average rate of return, had more than $2 *million* in their retirement account upon their death.

"I don't get it," he finally said.

"Before I explain, I have some more charts for you," Edward said. He pointed to the first chart he had showed Michael. This retiree averaged an 11.90 percent return over 25 years and wound up with $1.9 million. "The retiree retired in 1995 and passed away in 2019," Edward went on. "Again, not a bad time to retire. As you said, $1.9 million to the kids ain't bad."

Michael looked back down at the chart.

Change the retirement start date and your million dollars lasts

Retirement Year	Actual Year	Beginning Year Balance	Withdrawal	Post Withdrawal Balance	Return	End of Year Balance
1	1995	$1,000,000.00	$100,000.00	$900,000.00	38.02%	$1,242,180.00
2	1996	$1,242,180.00	$100,000.00	$1,142,180.00	23.06%	$1,405,566.71
3	1997	$1,405,566.71	$100,000.00	$1,305,566.71	33.67%	$1,745,151.02
4	1998	$1,745,151.02	$100,000.00	$1,645,151.02	28.73%	$2,117,802.91
5	1999	$2,117,802.91	$100,000.00	$2,017,802.91	21.11%	$2,443,761.10
6	2000	$2,443,761.10	$100,000.00	$2,343,761.10	-9.11%	$2,130,244.46
7	2001	$2,130,244.46	$100,000.00	$2,030,244.46	-11.98%	$1,787,021.18
8	2002	$1,787,021.18	$100,000.00	$1,687,021.18	-22.27%	$1,311,321.56
9	2003	$1,311,321.56	$100,000.00	$1,211,321.56	28.72%	$1,559,213.11
10	2004	$1,559,213.11	$100,000.00	$1,459,213.11	10.82%	$1,617,099.97
11	2005	$1,617,099.97	$100,000.00	$1,517,099.97	4.79%	$1,589,769.06
12	2006	$1,589,769.06	$100,000.00	$1,489,769.06	15.74%	$1,724,258.71
13	2007	$1,724,258.71	$100,000.00	$1,624,258.71	5.46%	$1,712,943.24
14	2008	$1,712,943.24	$100,000.00	$1,612,943.24	-37.22%	$1,012,605.76
15	2009	$1,012,605.76	$100,000.00	$912,605.76	27.11%	$1,160,013.19
16	2010	$1,160,013.19	$100,000.00	$1,060,013.19	14.87%	$1,217,637.15
17	2011	$1,217,637.15	$100,000.00	$1,117,637.15	2.07%	$1,140,772.24
18	2012	$1,140,772.24	$100,000.00	$1,040,772.24	15.88%	$1,206,046.87
19	2013	$1,206,046.87	$100,000.00	$1,106,046.87	32.43%	$1,464,737.87
20	2014	$1,464,737.87	$100,000.00	$1,364,737.87	13.81%	$1,553,208.17
21	2015	$1,553,208.17	$100,000.00	$1,453,208.17	1.31%	$1,472,245.19
22	2016	$1,472,245.19	$100,000.00	$1,372,245.19	11.93%	$1,535,954.04
23	2017	$1,535,954.04	$100,000.00	$1,435,954.04	21.94%	$1,751,002.36
24	2018	$1,751,002.36	$100,000.00	$1,651,002.36	-4.41%	$1,578,193.16
25	2019	$1,578,193.16	$100,000.00	$1,478,193.16	31.10%	$1,937,911.23
				Average	11.90%	

Figure 7.7

"But here is what happens when I reverse those years," Edward smiled. He slid the final chart across the table.

Reverse the start date and what do you notice?

Retirement Year	Actual Year	Beginning Year Balance	Withdrawal	Post Withdrawal Balance	S&P Return	End of Year Balance
1	2019	$1,000,000.00	$100,000.00	$900,000.00	31.10%	$1,179,900.00
2	2018	$1,179,900.00	$100,000.00	$1,079,900.00	-4.41%	$1,032,276.41
3	2017	$1,032,276.41	$100,000.00	$932,276.41	21.94%	$1,136,817.85
4	2016	$1,136,817.85	$100,000.00	$1,036,817.85	11.93%	$1,160,510.22
5	2015	$1,160,510.22	$100,000.00	$1,060,510.22	1.31%	$1,074,402.91
6	2014	$1,074,402.91	$100,000.00	$974,402.91	13.81%	$1,108,967.95
7	2013	$1,108,967.95	$100,000.00	$1,008,967.95	32.43%	$1,336,176.26
8	2012	$1,336,176.26	$100,000.00	$1,236,176.26	15.88%	$1,432,481.05
9	2011	$1,432,481.05	$100,000.00	$1,332,481.05	2.07%	$1,360,063.40
10	2010	$1,360,063.40	$100,000.00	$1,260,063.40	14.87%	$1,447,434.83
11	2009	$1,447,434.83	$100,000.00	$1,347,434.83	27.11%	$1,712,724.41
12	2008	$1,712,724.41	$100,000.00	$1,612,724.41	-37.22%	$1,012,468.39
13	2007	$1,012,468.39	$100,000.00	$912,468.39	5.46%	$962,289.16
14	2006	$962,289.16	$100,000.00	$862,289.16	15.74%	$998,013.48
15	2005	$998,013.48	$100,000.00	$898,013.48	4.79%	$941,028.32
16	2004	$941,028.32	$100,000.00	$841,028.32	10.82%	$932,027.58
17	2003	$932,027.58	$100,000.00	$832,027.58	28.72%	$1,070,985.91
18	2002	$1,070,985.91	$100,000.00	$970,985.91	-22.27%	$754,747.35
19	2001	$754,747.35	$100,000.00	$654,747.35	-11.98%	$576,308.61
20	2000	$576,308.61	$100,000.00	$476,308.61	-9.11%	$432,916.90
21	1999	$432,916.90	$100,000.00	$332,916.90	21.11%	$403,195.66
22	1998	$403,195.66	$100,000.00	$303,195.66	28.73%	$390,303.77
23	1997	$390,303.77	$100,000.00	$290,303.77	33.67%	$388,049.05
24	1996	$388,049.05	$100,000.00	$288,049.05	23.06%	$354,473.16
25	1995	$354,473.16	$100,000.00	$254,473.16	38.02%	$351,223.85
				Average	11.90%	

Figure 7.8

Michael saw that by reversing those years, that retiree still had $351,223.85 left over. But that was a far cry from the $1.9 *million* they had when retiring from 1995 to 2019.

"So with an average rate of return of 13.68 percent, and withdrawing only 10 percent of their original principal, one retiree has more than $2 million, while the other runs out of money in 13 years. And in another example, with an average rate of return of 11.90 percent, and again with-drawing only 10 percent of their original principal, one retiree has $1.9 million and the other has $351,000."

"Some pretty wild swings, right?" Kathleen said.

Edward nodded. "That's why average rates of return are the single most misleading calculation in all of personal finance. If someone plans their retirement around average rates of return, they run the risk of run-ning out of money. I used to tell my clients, it's like I have one foot in a bucket of 200-degree water and the other foot in a bucket of 0-degree water; on 'average' I should be comfortable, but in reality, I have two unhappy feet!"

Michael chuckled. He picked up his sandwich and took a bite. "So why does this happen? Why are there such wild swings in the results?"

"Let's take a look." Edward pointed to the chart of returns from 1972 to 2001. "Sam's troubles come at him right from the start. Just as he retires, the market has two negative years in a row. And we have to remember that his account value doesn't fall because of market losses alone; it also falls because he needs to withdraw money to live! Since he *has* to take out money, the account value drops in *half* by the third year."

> ## We have to remember that his account value doesn't fall because of market losses alone; it also falls because he needs to withdraw money to live!

"Retirement isn't looking so good," Michael said.

"You're right," Edward agreed. "But here's where things get really interesting. Markets generally *do* rebound and in years four and five they did just that. The market earned 38 percent and 24 percent respectively. Those are phenomenal returns. So what's the problem?"

Michael stared back down at the chart. He zeroed in on years four and five.

The dangers of withdrawing income during negative years

Retirement Year	Actual Year	Beginning Year Balance	Withdrawal	Post Withdrawal Balance	S&P Return	End of Year Balance
1	1972	$1,000,000.00	$100,000.00	$900,000.00	19.15%	$1,072,350.00
2	1973	$1,072,350.00	$100,000.00	$972,350.00	-15.03%	$826,205.80
3	1974	$826,205.80	$100,000.00	$726,205.80	-26.95%	$530,493.33
4	1975	$530,493.33	$100,000.00	$430,493.33	38.46%	$596,061.07
5	1976	$596,061.07	$100,000.00	$496,061.07	24.20%	$616,107.85

Figure 7.9

Then it hit him.

"The returns might be great," Michael said as he pointed to the paper. "But the value is *half* of what Sam started with. He's not earning 38 percent on the original $1 million, he's earning it on only $530,493."

"Right," Edward continued. "Even though the market had a nice rebound, it did not rebound on the *original* balance. The growth is not high enough to withstand constantly taking out $100,000. He is now in a downward spiral that will eventually leave him penniless. When we use the 'average rate of return' we *think* we are going to retire in style. But when we use *actual* returns, we discover we are flat broke!"

It is hard to recover your money even in good years

Retirement Year	Actual Year	Beginning Year Balance	Withdrawal	Post Withdrawal Balance	Return	End of Year Balance
1	1972	$1,000,000.00	$100,000.00	$900,000.00	19.15%	$1,072,350.00
2	1973	$1,072,350.00	$100,000.00	$972,350.00	-15.03%	$826,205.80
3	1974	$826,205.80	$100,000.00	$726,205.80	-26.95%	$530,493.33
4	1975	$530,493.33	$100,000.00	$430,493.33	38.46%	$596,061.07
5	1976	$596,061.07	$100,000.00	$496,061.07	24.20%	$616,107.85
6	1977	$616,107.85	$100,000.00	$516,107.85	-7.78%	$475,954.66
7	1978	$475,954.66	$100,000.00	$375,954.66	6.41%	$400,053.35
8	1979	$400,053.35	$100,000.00	$300,053.35	18.69%	$356,133.32
9	1980	$356,133.32	$100,000.00	$256,133.32	32.67%	$339,812.08

Figure 7.10

The truth hit Michael like a ton of bricks. "That's what Jill's father is constantly afraid of," Michael said. "Running out of money."

Kathleen speared some salad. "He is right to be worried. The *single* fastest way to run out of money is to take a withdrawal when the market is negative."

The *single* fastest way to run out of money is to take a withdrawal when the market is negative.

Michael set the chart on the picnic table and let the magnitude of the situation settle. He wondered how a person could *ever* plan for their retirement.

His father interrupted his thoughts. "The problem has many names. It's sometimes referred to as *reverse dollar-cost averaging* or *erosion of principal.* But the term I use most often is *sequence-of-return risk.* It is an unspoken risk in the financial planning community. We all know about volatility risk—the markets go up and down. To an investor, the ups and downs are just how it goes. But to a *retiree* who *has* to withdraw money, the *sequence* of returns is crucial. Few people have ever heard of sequence-of-return risk, but it's there, staring us right in the face, and it can devastate even the strongest of retirement plans."

Few people have ever heard of sequence-of-return risk, but it's there, staring us right in the face, and it can devastate even the strongest of retirement plans.

They ate in silence for a few minutes, until Edward spoke. "Will you permit me just a couple more charts?"

"Dad, this is too many charts for a Saturday." Michael cupped his head in his hands.

"Last two, I promise. We established that if we take our returns and reverse them, we get drastically different outcomes. Even though the average rates of return are the same, the final dollar amounts couldn't be further apart."

"Sure," Michael said.

"But those results are from reversing the returns. Let me show you just how much difference even *one* year can make using the same sequence of returns one year apart. Imagine a family of brothers and sisters—our retiree, Sam, and his siblings Joe, Bob, and Sally. They all retire with $1 million, and they retire one year after their next oldest sibling. Sam, the oldest, retires first, followed by his brother Joe, who is followed up by his brother Bob, and their sister Sally brings up the rear. See for yourself the difference one year can make."

THE 5TH OPTION

Sam
Retires in 1972 with $1 million

Retirement Year	Actual Year	Beginning Year Balance	Withdrawal	Post Withdrawal Balance	S&P Return	End of Year Balance
1	1972	$1,000,000.00	$100,000.00	$900,000.00	19.15%	$1,070,460.00
2	1973	$1,070,460.00	$100,000.00	$970,460.00	-15.03%	$826,928.97
3	1974	$826,928.97	$100,000.00	$726,928.97	-26.95%	$534,002.02
4	1975	$534,002.02	$100,000.00	$434,002.02	38.46%	$595,667.77
5	1976	$595,667.77	$100,000.00	$495,667.77	24.20%	$612,992.33
6	1977	$612,992.33	$100,000.00	$512,992.33	-7.78%	$475,082.20
7	1978	$475,082.20	$100,000.00	$375,082.20	6.41%	$399,237.49
8	1979	$399,237.49	$100,000.00	$299,237.49	18.69%	$354,147.57
9	1980	$354,147.57	$100,000.00	$254,147.57	32.67%	$336,160.99
10	1981	$336,160.99	$100,000.00	$236,160.99	-5.33%	$224,234.86
11	1982	$224,234.86	$100,000.00	$124,234.86	21.22%	$150,920.51
12	1983	$150,920.51	$100,000.00	$50,920.51	23.13%	$62,377.63
13	1984	$62,377.63	$100,000.00	$0	5.96%	$0
14	1985	$0	$100,000.00	$0	32.24%	$0
15	1986	$0	$100,000.00	$0	19.06%	$0
16	1987	$0	$100,000.00	$0	5.69%	$0
17	1988	$0	$100,000.00	$0	16.64%	$0
18	1989	$0	$100,000.00	$0	32.00%	$0
19	1990	$0	$100,000.00	$0	-3.42%	$0
20	1991	$0	$100,000.00	$0	30.95%	$0
21	1992	$0	$100,000.00	$0	7.60%	$0
22	1993	$0	$100,000.00	$0	10.17%	$0
23	1994	$0	$100,000.00	$0	1.19%	$0
24	1995	$0	$100,000.00	$0	38.02%	$0
25	1996	$0	$100,000.00	$0	23.06%	$0
26	1997	$0	$100,000.00	$0	33.67%	$0
27	1998	$0	$100,000.00	$0	28.73%	$0
28	1999	$0	$100,000.00	$0	21.11%	$0
29	2000	$0	$100,000.00	$0	-9.11%	$0
30	2001	$0	$100,000.00	$0	-11.98%	$0

Joe
Retires in 1973 with $1 million

Retirement Year	Actual Year	Beginning Year Balance	Withdrawal	Post Withdrawal Balance	S&P Return	End of Year Balance
1	1972				19.15%	
2	1973	$1,000,000.00	$100,000.00	$900,000.00	-15.03%	$766,890.00
3	1974	$766,890.00	$100,000.00	$666,890.00	-26.95%	$489,897.39
4	1975	$489,897.39	$100,000.00	$389,897.39	38.46%	$535,134.17
5	1976	$535,134.17	$100,000.00	$435,134.17	24.20%	$538,130.43
6	1977	$538,130.43	$100,000.00	$438,130.43	-7.78%	$405,752.59
7	1978	$405,752.59	$100,000.00	$305,752.59	6.41%	$325,443.06
8	1979	$325,443.06	$100,000.00	$225,443.06	18.69%	$266,811.86
9	1980	$266,811.86	$100,000.00	$166,811.86	32.67%	$220,642.05
10	1981	$220,642.05	$100,000.00	$120,642.05	-5.33%	$114,549.63
11	1982	$114,549.63	$100,000.00	$14,549.63	21.22%	$17,674.89
12	1983	$17,674.89	$100,000.00	$0	23.13%	$0
13	1984	$0	$100,000.00	$0	5.96%	$0
14	1985	$0	$100,000.00	$0	32.24%	$0
15	1986	$0	$100,000.00	$0	19.06%	$0
16	1987	$0	$100,000.00	$0	5.69%	$0
17	1988	$0	$100,000.00	$0	16.64%	$0
18	1989	$0	$100,000.00	$0	32.00%	$0
19	1990	$0	$100,000.00	$0	-3.42%	$0
20	1991	$0	$100,000.00	$0	30.95%	$0
21	1992	$0	$100,000.00	$0	7.60%	$0
22	1993	$0	$100,000.00	$0	10.17%	$0
23	1994	$0	$100,000.00	$0	1.19%	$0
24	1995	$0	$100,000.00	$0	38.02%	$0
25	1996	$0	$100,000.00	$0	23.06%	$0
26	1997	$0	$100,000.00	$0	33.67%	$0
27	1998	$0	$100,000.00	$0	28.73%	$0
28	1999	$0	$100,000.00	$0	21.11%	$0
29	2000	$0	$100,000.00	$0	-9.11%	$0
30	2001	$0	$100,000.00	$0	-11.98%	$0

Bob
Retires in 1974 with $1 million

Retirement Year	Actual Year	Beginning Year Balance	Withdrawal	Post Withdrawal Balance	S&P Return	End of Year Balance
1	1972				19.15%	
2	1973				**-15.03%**	
3	1974	$1,000,000.00	$100,000.00	$900,000.00	**-26.95%**	$661,140.00
4	1975	$661,140.00	$100,000.00	$561,140.00	38.46%	$770,164.65
5	1976	$770,164.65	$100,000.00	$670,164.65	24.20%	$828,792.62
6	1977	$828,792.62	$100,000.00	$728,792.62	**-7.78%**	$674,934.85
7	1978	$674,934.85	$100,000.00	$574,934.85	6.41%	$611,960.65
8	1979	$611,960.65	$100,000.00	$511,960.65	18.69%	$605,905.43
9	1980	$605,905.43	$100,000.00	$505,905.43	32.67%	$669,161.11
10	1981	$669,161.11	$100,000.00	$569,161.11	**-5.33%**	$540,418.48
11	1982	$540,418.48	$100,000.00	$440,418.48	21.22%	$535,020.37
12	1983	$535,020.37	$100,000.00	$435,020.37	23.13%	$532,899.95
13	1984	$532,899.95	$100,000.00	$432,899.95	5.96%	$459,523.30
14	1985	$459,523.30	$100,000.00	$359,523.30	32.24%	$473,312.42
15	1986	$473,312.42	$100,000.00	$373,312.42	19.06%	$442,748.53
16	1987	$442,748.53	$100,000.00	$342,748.53	5.69%	$360,468.63
17	1988	$360,468.63	$100,000.00	$260,468.63	16.64%	$303,732.47
18	1989	$303,732.47	$100,000.00	$203,732.47	32.00%	$268,295.29
19	1990	$268,295.29	$100,000.00	$168,295.29	**-3.42%**	$163,078.13
20	1991	$163,078.13	$100,000.00	$63,078.13	30.95%	$82,298.04
21	1991	$82,298.04	$100,000.00	$0	7.60%	$0
22	1993	$0	$100,000.00	$0	10.17%	$0
23	1994	$0	$100,000.00	$0	1.19%	$0
24	1995	$0	$100,000.00	$0	38.02%	$0
25	1996	$0	$100,000.00	$0	23.06%	$0
26	1997	$0	$100,000.00	$0	33.67%	$0
27	1998	$0	$100,000.00	$0	28.73%	$0
28	1999	$0	$100,000.00	$0	21.11%	$0
29	2000	$0	$100,000.00	$0	**-9.11%**	$0
30	2001	$0	$100,000.00	$0	**-11.98%**	$0

Sally
Retires in 1975 with $1 million

Retirement Year	Actual Year	Beginning Year Balance	Withdrawal	Post Withdrawal Balance	S&P Return	End of Year Balance
1	1972				19.15%	
2	1973				-15.03%	
3	1974				-26.95%	
4	1975	$1,000,000.00	$100,000.00	$900,000.00	38.46%	$1,235,250.00
5	1976	$1,235,250.00	$100,000.00	$1,135,250.00	24.20%	$1,403,963.68
6	1977	$1,403,963.68	$100,000.00	$1,303,963.68	-7.78%	$1,207,600.76
7	1978	$1,207,600.76	$100,000.00	$1,107,600.76	6.41%	$1,178,930.25
8	1979	$1,178,930.25	$100,000.00	$1,078,930.25	18.69%	$1,276,913.95
9	1980	$1,276,913.95	$100,000.00	$1,176,913.95	32.67%	$1,556,704.08
10	1981	$1,556,704.08	$100,000.00	$1,456,704.08	-5.33%	$1,383,140.52
11	1982	$1,383,140.52	$100,000.00	$1,283,140.52	21.22%	$1,558,759.11
12	1983	$1,558,759.11	$100,000.00	$1,458,759.11	23.13%	$1,786,979.91
13	1984	$1,786,979.91	$100,000.00	$1,686,979.91	5.96%	$1,790,729.17
14	1985	$1,790,729.17	$100,000.00	$1,690,729.17	32.24%	$2,225,844.96
15	1986	$2,225,844.96	$100,000.00	$2,125,844.96	19.06%	$2,521,252.12
16	1987	$2,521,252.12	$100,000.00	$2,421,252.12	5.69%	$2,546,430.85
17	1988	$2,546,430.85	$100,000.00	$2,446,430.85	16.64%	$2,852,783.02
18	1989	$2,852,783.02	$100,000.00	$2,752,783.02	32.00%	$3,625,139.95
19	1990	$3,625,139.95	$100,000.00	$3,525,139.95	-3.42%	$3,415,860.62
20	1991	$3,415,860.62	$100,000.00	$3,315,860.62	30.95%	$4,326,203.35
21	1992	$4,326,203.35	$100,000.00	$4,226,203.35	7.60%	$4,548,240.04
22	1993	$4,548,240.04	$100,000.00	$4,448,240.04	10.17%	$4,896,622.64
23	1994	$4,896,622.64	$100,000.00	$4,796,622.64	1.19%	$4,859,938.06
24	1995	$4,859,938.06	$100,000.00	$4,759,938.06	38.02%	$6,548,722.78
25	1996	$6,548,722.78	$100,000.00	$6,448,722.78	23.06%	$7,929,349.53
26	1997	$7,929,349.53	$100,000.00	$7,829,349.53	33.67%	$10,441,220.53
27	1998	$10,441,220.53	$100,000.00	$10,341,220.53	28.73%	$13,296,741.35
28	1999	$13,296,741.35	$100,000.00	$13,196,741.35	21.11%	$15,973,335.73
29	2000	$15,973,335.73	$100,000.00	$15,873,335.73	-9.11%	$14,428,862.18
30	2001	$14,428,862.18	$100,000.00	$14,328,862.18	-11.98%	$12,625,160.47

Figure 7.11

"Wow," Michael said. "What a difference a year can make."

"It's not the year," Edward corrected him. "It's the sequence that you get *from* the year you decide to retire. The sequence is what we cannot control, and it's *that* sequence, coupled with longevity risk, that forces us into a retirement plan we do not like."

"So we are all on the retirement desert island, unsure of when it will rain and how long before we are rescued. We are forced to drink the smallest amounts of money possible," Michael said.

"That's right. When you retire, who will you be? Will you be Sam who dies with $1.7 million of debt? Or Joe with $1.8 million dollars of debt? Or will you be Bob or the super lucky Sally?"

Michael shook his head. "There's just no way to know."

"Stressing and guessing," Kathleen said.

"That's right. If Sam *knew* he would only live 10 years, then his plan works just fine. If Joe *knew* he was going to die in his 12th year of retirement, he'd be fine too. But he has no way of knowing."

"Longevity risk," Michael said. He fell silent. *How had things gotten to this?* He and Jill had been working with the same financial advisor for years, but that advisor never mentioned sequence-of-return risk. Even he himself, an avid reader of financial blogs, had never heard of it. It irritated him that he had been investing so long with such an unknown risk.

He crossed his arms and furrowed his brow. "Okay. I see the problem trying to use average rates of return to predict retirement income. In this example, Sam was trying to take out $100,000 a year, or 10 percent of his portfolio's beginning value. We know that 10 percent didn't work for him. But what about 9 percent? Or even 8 percent? Maybe those numbers would work?"

Edward finished his last bite of food. "The financial planning industry asked that very same question. Specifically, *'What is the highest percentage of a retiree's portfolio they can withdraw every year without running out of money?'*"

"Let me guess, the answer isn't pleasant?"

Edward nodded. "It's bad, and it's getting worse."

Michael's Notebook:

- Average rates of return DO NOT equal yearly actual *rates of return*.
  - ◊ This is why if you average a 9 percent return you **CANNOT** take out 8 percent per year.
  - ◊ This is called *sequence-of-return risk* (a.k.a. volatility risk).
- The *single* fastest way to run out of money is to take a withdrawal when the market is negative.
- A few negative market years can wipe out a person's retirement.
- Even retiring a year or two later or earlier can change everything.
- How much can we take out?

CHAPTER 8

THE BENGEN RULE

M ichael and Kathleen started on the western side of the barn, while their father cleaned up after lunch. As he painted, Michael thought about how he had gotten here.

He was beginning to see the complexity of retirement planning. There was a lot more to this than he thought. For years he and Jill had been playing it simple: Just save as much money as possible. But he didn't realize just how *much* they had to save, because of longevity risk and sequence-of-return risk. He was convinced now more than ever that he and Jill needed to get more money into their retirement accounts. Those expensive life insurance policies had to go.

When Michael's father had finished cleaning up, they were back in their usual positions. Michael's father on the ground, Michael on the short ladder, and his sister on the tall ladder near the roofline.

His father began with a quick review.

"You now know that while big piles of money are helpful in our retirement accounts, we are *always* going to be victim to the two great unknowns. We never know how long we are going to live, and we never know what sequence of returns we are going to get. If you could know how long you were going to live, and if you could know what *order* of returns you will earn in retirement, it would be simple to plan. The problem is that's impossible to know. Some folks will get lucky, others will not."

We never know how long we are going to live, and we never know what sequence of returns we are going to get.

Michael nodded, recalling the chart of the Smith family, each of whom retired with $1 million, just a year apart. Sam, who retired first, would have been $1.7 million in debt at the end of his retirement.[1] Sally, who retired last, would have been able to leave $12 million to her kids. He had been baffled by the enormous swings in just a few short years.

"Since we cannot predict our sequence of returns and since we cannot know how long we are going to live, the financial planning industry came up with the systematic withdrawal strategy," Edward said.

"Yes, our advisor mentioned that strategy," Michael said.

"It is the typical default retirement plan that most traditional financial advisors suggest. The strategy consists of growing the biggest balance sheet possible in your working years and then, in your retirement years, selling the assets on that balance sheet to create a yearly income.[2] The question is, what percentage of your assets can you sell every year and still be sure you don't run out of money?"

"Just like the person on the desert island trying to figure out how much they can drink every day," Kathleen chimed in, "the financial planning industry is trying to figure out how much we can withdraw every year."

"Exactly," Edward said. "Over the years, the financial planning industry has run thousands of scenarios to determine a safe withdrawal rate for the systematic withdrawal strategy—basically a percentage of your nest egg that you can 'safely' withdraw every year without running out of money.

"The trouble—as you're beginning to see—is that converting assets into income isn't as easy as it appears. We've seen that the sequence of our market returns plays a major role in our chances of success. We also learned that a retiree has no idea how long they will need their money to last. Because of longevity risk and volatility—or sequence-of-return—risk, the systematic withdrawal strategy forces ultra-conservative withdrawals.

> **The trouble—as you're beginning to see—is that converting assets into income isn't as easy as it appears.**

"We have to remember that the idea of a safe withdrawal rate didn't exist during the golden age of pensions. For most people, pensions, Social Security, and just a little bit from personal savings were adequate to live on. But today's world is different. As pensions disappeared, retirees not only needed to rely more on their own investments, they also had to figure out how to safely convert their balance sheets into income. The financial planning industry had to answer that key question: *What percentage of my balance sheet can I sell every year and still be sure I don't run out of money?*"

> **The financial planning industry had to answer that key question: *What percentage of my balance sheet can I sell every year and still be sure I don't run out of money?***

Kathleen had descended the ladder, and Edward helped her move it to a new spot. When she had safely returned to painting the roofline, Edward continued. "In 1994, someone decided to dig a little deeper. William Bengen was a financial planner who reviewed historical market data. He wanted to determine what percentage of a person's retirement account they could withdraw every year and be sure they would not run out of money over a 30-year period.

"Bengen looked at rolling 30-year periods of the stock market, beginning in 1926. He began running calculations on hypothetical scenarios, testing different withdrawal rates against different portfolios during different 30-year periods. He was looking for the highest withdrawal rate that would still ensure a person would not run out of money."

Edward set down his paintbrush and looked at his son. "Bengen called his conclusion the 'Safe Max Rate,' and, sadly, the highest rate he found that would not fail was 4 percent."

"Four percent? Yeah, I've heard about the 4 percent rule before. Well, at least that's better than what our advisor was talking about."

"Sit tight," Kathleen said. "It gets *worse*."

Michael turned to his father. "*Worse?*"

"We have to remember, son, that Bengen's research was originally conducted in 1994. Since then, two events have happened that have changed the safe withdrawal rate. The first was an unprecedented lowering of interest rates. Of course, lower interest rates are wonderful for people trying to borrow money, but they can be hard on retirees looking for fixed incomes. It is much more difficult to build a fixed-income portfolio in a low-interest rate environment.

"The second event was the rise in the average life expectancy. People are living longer, and they need to make their money last for a longer period of time.

"So now the financial planning industry believes the new safe withdrawal rate is closer to 3 percent. The academic world considers it even lower: 2.7 percent."[3]

Michael folded his arms on the top of the ladder, stunned at what his father just told him. "You said 2.7 percent? That cannot be right."

"I know it seems crazy. It's not what you expected; it's *nowhere* near what you expected.

"Millions of Americans have been led to believe that in order for their retirements to work out, they just need to get a big enough balance sheet. There is tremendous pressure to save more and more. The danger is that this strategy *feels* like it works. Get a big balance sheet. Then earn an average rate of return on that balance sheet. Then withdraw less than your average rate of return. People ask, 'how could that *not* work?'

Millions of Americans have been led to believe that in order for their retirements to work out, they just need to get a big enough balance sheet.

"When it comes time to convert that big balance sheet into *income*, however, the trouble is revealed. That's when people learn about the safe withdrawal rate and how little their retirement income will be. This is why I call it B.S. retirement planning. If we don't plan for cash flow, all we have is our balance sheet, and the balance sheet alone cannot get us the income we want."

Michael shook his head. "I'm sorry, but I don't buy it. Three percent is just too low. And 2.7 percent is ridiculous. I get that the withdrawal rate needs to be safe to ensure you don't run out of money. But I think you could get away withdrawing more than that. Why not 6 percent?"

"Great question. And you're certainly not the first person to ask it. Ever since Bengen's 4 percent rule, the financial planning industry has asked that very same question *thousands* of times: *What is the highest rate a person can withdraw from their retirement account so that they do not run out of money over a 30-year period?*

"To answer that, the financial planning industry has run thousands of computer simulations on thousands of portfolio allocations with different sequences of annual returns. Essentially, the industry was trying to calculate the likelihood that a person would not run out of money.

"Remember, when pensions went away, retirement planning shifted from guarantees to chance. From firm ground to quicksand. In order to minimize the damage of this shift, the financial planning industry had to figure out a safe withdrawal rate."

Remember, when pensions went away, retirement planning shifted from guarantees to chance.

Edward laid down his paintbrush. "Come off that ladder, and let me show you something." He looked up at his daughter. "Kath, you need a break?"

"Nah, I'm good. You two talk."

Michael set down his brush and joined his father at the picnic table. The pitcher of iced tea was half full and still cold. Michael refilled his glass and sat.

"I want you to look at this." Edward removed a few sheets of paper from his briefcase and handed Michael the first one.

"This chart was created by a computer program called Monte Carlo. The program makes predictions about the likelihood of an event. Researchers used the program to run thousands of sample retirement portfolios with thousands of different possibilities. They varied the historical amount of returns and the asset allocations between stocks and bonds.

"This chart is from a simulation of a retirement portfolio consisting of 100 percent stocks," Edward said. "I'll bet your advisor used a chart like that when he broke that bad news to you and Jill about how little you could withdraw. The chart predicts your chances of running out of money over a 30-year retirement, based on various withdrawal rates."

Michael studied the chart. He traced his finger along the 7 percent withdrawal line. "So, if I withdraw 7 percent per year, then there is just under a 70 percent chance I will *not* run out of money in the 20th year?" Michael looked up at his father. "So that means there is a 30 percent chance I *will* run out of money?"

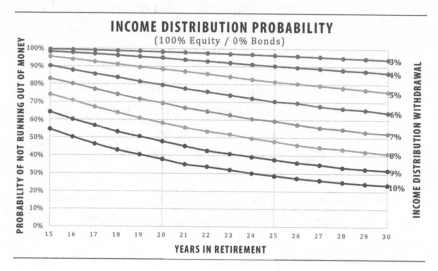

Figure 8.1. Source: Shah Asnari Kinetic Financial

"I'm afraid so. And as you can see, the longer your retirement, the higher your chances of running out of money at any rate, even at the suggested 3 percent."

Michael quickly grasped that the chart revealed several frightening facts about retirement planning. The first is that the higher the withdrawal rate, the more likely a person will run out of money. The second is that when a retirement lasts longer than 25 years, the chances of running out of money start to *drastically* increase.

And the third revelation, perhaps the most frightening, was that even at a 3 percent withdrawal rate, there was *still* a chance a person could run out of money. It was simply a question of what percent chance of failure a retiree was comfortable with. Whatever withdrawal rate a person chose, it *might* all work out. But, as Michael recalled from the four siblings of the Smith family, just *one* year could unravel it all.

Then an idea hit him. "Hold up, Dad." He pointed at the chart. "This portfolio is 100 percent stocks. Wouldn't retirees be more diversified?"

Edward grinned. His son's question was a common belief, one he'd heard many times. "The problem with that thinking is that modern retirements can last 30 years or more. A person needs at least *some* growth with a timeline that long.

"I know it seems counterintuitive, but people who have too much money in safer investments—like bonds and CDs—run the risk of running out of money *faster than those who still have some money in stocks* because they don't get the growth they need," Edward explained.

"They run out of money *faster?*"

"They do."

Edward handed another chart to his son. This chart revealed the probabilities of running out of money for a retiree with a portfolio of 50 percent stocks and 50 percent bonds.

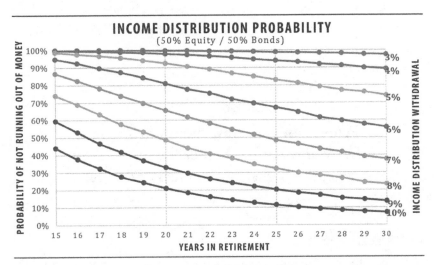

Figure 8.2. Source: Shah Asnari Kinetic Financial

He watched as Michael placed his finger along the 8 percent withdrawal line of the 50/50 portfolio chart. At that withdrawal rate, there was only a 25 percent chance of NOT running out of money. Michael then drew his finger along the 6 percent line and found there was *still* only a 55 percent chance of not running out of money.

"This is why the withdrawal rate has to be *super* low," Edward said. "We just don't know how long we will live or what sequence of returns we will get."

Michael put down the chart and exhaled. "It's crazy. It's like we're being asked to get on an airplane that *might* not land."

"That's right." Edward patted his arm. "Would you board a plane if the pilot said, 'Welcome aboard Retirement Airlines. We expect a smooth flight and we calculate that we have a 78 percent chance of making it to Hawaii?'"

"Heck no."

"How about if there was an 82 percent chance of making it to Hawaii?"

"Again, no."

"I agree. But sadly, this is the choice many people are making with their retirements. They can withdraw money at any rate they want, but the higher the withdrawal rate, the higher the chances of failure. But since the safe withdrawal rate is so low, there is tremendous pressure to increase retirement income another way."

People can withdraw money at any rate they want, but the higher the withdrawal rate, the higher the chances of failure.

"Like the four options?" Michael asked.

"Exactly," Edward said. "People fall victim to the Frustrating Four. Big barrel, small sips."

Edward smiled. He had had this conversation with many people before, and it was his favorite part.

"It doesn't have to be that way, son. We are simply trying to solve the problem from the wrong end. When we move beyond the systematic withdrawal strategy then everything changes."

"How do we do that?"

"Hey there!" Kathleen walked up to them. She counted off on her four fingers, then she folded in those fingers and stuck out her thumb.

Michael smiled. "The Fifth Option."

Michael's Notebook:

- With erosion of pensions, the financial planning industry had to answer the key question: *What percent of my assets can I sell every year without fear of running out of money?*

- In 1994 William Bengen's research revealed 4 percent was the safe withdrawal rate.

- But today interest rates are lower, and life expectancies are longer.

- The NEW rate is 3 percent or LESS!!

- Withdraw any higher and the chances of failure increase.

- Four options:

  ◊ Work longer

  ◊ Save more

  ◊ More risk

  ◊ Cut back

- **The Fifth Option** = moving beyond the systematic withdrawal strategy. But HOW???

CHAPTER 9

BEAT THE BEAR

M ichael was more than ready to find out what the Fifth Option was, but when he asked his sister, she winked and told him, "I think you've been hit with enough information for one day." Michael protested, "But . . . "

Edward cupped his hand over Michael's shoulder. "Kathleen's right. Let's call it a day."

Michael begged Kathleen three more times on the long drive home, but she deftly dodged the topic and switched to a new one each time until Michael found himself outside of his house, no closer to a solution for his and Jill's retirement. Nevertheless, Michael somehow felt more at ease than he had since the meeting with their financial planner. Whatever the Fifth Option was, it carried with it a hint of hope and possibility. And right now Michael needed to believe that something existed beyond the Frustrating Four.

* * *

When the kids were in bed, and Michael and Jill were getting ready for bed themselves, Michael told his wife about what he had learned from his sister and father that day. Jill listened as she brushed her teeth. When he finished, Jill abruptly finished brushing and turned to Michael with her eyes wide.

"Wow! So a few early down years could wipe us out. And we won't know when the down years are coming, and we won't know how many we'll have to endure." Jill spat out the rest of her toothpaste. "So it makes sense that we would have to be more conservative than we initially thought with the amount of income we can withdraw to ensure we don't run out of money."

Jill took a glass of water and rinsed her mouth. She grabbed a hairbrush and walked out of the bathroom, brushing away.

"What I did *not* expect is just how low that withdrawal amount needs to be. What really frustrates me is that whichever option we choose, it *still* might not be enough."

Michael followed her and sat on the chair in their bedroom. "Doing it the way we are currently doing it, with the systematic withdrawal strategy, then it's possible we'll run out of money. And the more money we take out, the more likely we are to run out."

Jill pulled back the blanket and sheets on the bed. "But there *is* a Fifth Option?"

"Apparently there is. Apparently it's possible to safely increase the withdrawal rate so our retirement incomes will be higher, *and* we can have the retirement we want."

"I really hope so." Jill climbed into bed. "I do not like the path we are on."

Michael joined her on the other side of the bed and turned off the lamp. "I agree. I'll learn how tomorrow."

* * *

The next morning, Kathleen again picked Michael up at nine, and they drove to their father's house. Michael was glad he could help his father paint the barn, but his mind was mostly occupied with wondering about the Fifth Option. He smiled as he looked out the window. He was beginning to see that the old man knew a heck of a lot more than he let on.

When the car pulled up, Michael saw his father had already laid out the tarps and carried all the paint and brushes to the east side of the barn. He also noticed the picnic table had a thermos of coffee and a basket of muffins.

"I figured we'd start with a coffee break," Edward smiled.

"I like that schedule," Michael grinned.

The three of them sat down and filled their mugs with coffee. As he took a muffin from the basket, Michael noticed the leather briefcase from yesterday at his father's side.

"Alright," Edward began, "Michael, you now know the challenge in modern retirement planning. With the disappearance of pensions, most of us are on our own to fund our retirement needs, potentially for a very long time. Without pensions, we have to plan our retirements without knowing two factors."

"Longevity and sequence of returns," Michael said.

"Correct," Edward said. "When we use the systematic withdrawal strategy, the only way to protect against longevity and sequence-of-return risk is to lower the withdrawal rate. Obviously, the reason you are here is because the rate your advisor suggested is nowhere near what you had in mind."

"You got that right."

"The good news is that there is a Fifth Option, outside of the Frustrating Four, and it focuses on safely moving beyond the systematic withdrawal strategy. I'm going show you three alternative strategies that can do just that. Remember the goal of *all* of these strategies is to optimize retirement income."

Edward pointed his finger. "Sacrificing and saving more money to get more income is B.S. retirement thinking. Yes, you have to save money. That is true. But the goal of these strategies is to create safe, predictable, and plentiful income. I think you'll find that among the three strategies, there will be one that will accommodate every retiree's preferences. If, for example, a retiree likes the markets—the lure of a big upside—there is a strategy for that person. Other people will want a hands-off approach, with as little market interaction as possible. Well, there's a strategy for that, too. And there is a strategy that is right in the middle."

"Okay," Michael said, "so where do we start?"

"We start by revisiting why we're even considering alternative retirement strategies," Edward said. "You remember yesterday when we discussed our hypothetical retiree, Sam?" Edward slid a chart across the table. "Sam retired in 1972. Sadly, the sequence of returns wasn't very kind to him."

Will your million dollars last if you average 13.68%?

Retirement Year	Actual Year	Beginning Year Balance	Withdrawal	Post Withdrawal Balance	S&P Return	End of Year Balance
1	1972	$1,000,000.00	$100,000.00	$900,000.00	19.15%	$1,072,350.00
2	1973	$1,072,350.00	$100,000.00	$972,350.00	-15.03%	$826,205.80
3	1974	$826,205.80	$100,000.00	$726,205.80	-26.95%	$530,493.33
4	1975	$530,493.33	$100,000.00	$430,493.33	38.46%	$596,061.07
5	1976	$596,061.07	$100,000.00	$496,061.07	24.20%	$616,107.85
6	1977	$616,107.85	$100,000.00	$516,107.85	-7.78%	$475,954.66
7	1978	$475,954.66	$100,000.00	$375,954.66	6.41%	$400,053.35
8	1979	$400,053.35	$100,000.00	$300,053.35	18.69%	$356,133.32
9	1980	$356,133.32	$100,000.00	$256,133.32	32.67%	$339,812.08
10	1981	$339,812.08	$100,000.00	$239,812.08	-5.33%	$227,030.09
11	1982	$227,030.09	$100,000.00	$127,030.09	21.22%	$153,985.88
12	1983	$153,985.88	$100,000.00	$53,985.88	23.13%	$66,472.82
13	1984	$66,472.82	$100,000.00	$0	5.96%	$0
14	1985	$0	$100,000.00	$0	32.24%	$0
15	1986	$0	$100,000.00	$0	19.06%	$0
16	1987	$0	$100,000.00	$0	5.69%	$0
17	1988	$0	$100,000.00	$0	16.64%	$0
18	1989	$0	$100,000.00	$0	32.00%	$0
19	1990	$0	$100,000.00	$0	-3.42%	$0
20	1991	$0	$100,000.00	$0	30.95%	$0
21	1992	$0	$100,000.00	$0	7.60%	$0
22	1993	$0	$100,000.00	$0	10.17%	$0
23	1994	$0	$100,000.00	$0	1.19%	$0
24	1995	$0	$100,000.00	$0	38.02%	$0
25	1996	$0	$100,000.00	$0	23.06%	$0
26	1997	$0	$100,000.00	$0	33.67%	$0
27	1998	$0	$100,000.00	$0	28.73%	$0
28	1999	$0	$100,000.00	$0	21.11%	$0
29	2000	$0	$100,000.00	$0	-9.11%	$0
30	2001	$0	$100,000.00	$0	-11.98%	$0
			Average Rate of Return		13.68%	

Figure 9.1

Michael nodded. Sam had retired with $1 million and wanted to take out $100,000 a year, or 10 percent of his original retirement account. Even though Sam *averaged* an impressive 13.68 percent return, he ran out of money in 13 years.

Michael threw up his hands. "It just feels like retirement is a kind of roulette wheel."

"Stressing and guessing," Kathleen said.

"The uncertainty must drive retirees nuts," Michael said.

Edward seemed to look past them, as if recalling clients from long ago. "People drive themselves crazy with questions like, *Is it okay to go on this $3,000 vacation? What if I have a $10,000 emergency? I know I can afford this item today, but will buying it cause me to run out of money faster?* Trying to figure out how much to save and how much to withdraw is *literally* the most stressful guessing game of your life, because you can't afford to get it wrong."

Trying to figure out how much to save and how much to withdraw is *literally* the most stressful guessing game of your life, because you can't afford to get it wrong.

"So people just live on the smallest amount possible? Big barrel, small sips?"

Edward turned back to Michael. "You just never know, son." His father slid a familiar chart in front of him. Even at a low rate like 3 percent, there was *still* a chance the money would run out.

He tapped the chart. "How much risk do you feel comfortable taking?"

How much risk do you feel comfortable taking?

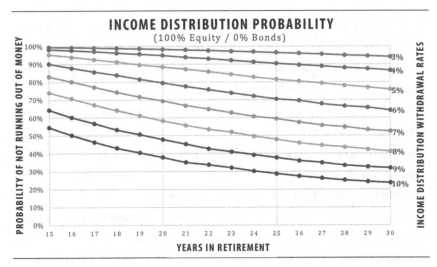

Figure 9.2. Source: Shah Ansari Kinetic Financial

Michael just stared into his cup of coffee. "I guess I am seeing that in real time with Jill's father. I now understand why he acts the way he does. He knows a $3,000 vacation taken in year two of his retirement might just result in him running out of money in year 15."

He looked up at his father and sister. "I don't want to live like that. But I *also* don't want to limit my withdrawals to an unbearably low rate."

"Sadly, that is the financial planning industry's solution," Edward said. "Of course, you could take out more money. And depending on the sequence of returns you get, it might all work. You might end up with millions, like Sally did in our example. Or you might run out of money halfway through."

"But even Sally doesn't have the retirement she wants," Kathleen jumped in. "Think about this in real life. When someone retires, when are they *most* active? When are they most physically able to do the things they want?"

Michael thought for a moment. "For most people I would say in their early retirement years. The older you get, the harder it is to travel and be active."

"That's right. Early on in retirement is when retirees are most physically active. They are able to travel, bike, hike, play golf, whatever. But those early years are also when a retiree needs to be the most *financially* cautious. We've seen just how devastating a bad stock market year can be, especially one that occurs at the beginning of retirement. So the years that retirees are most *physically* able to get out and experience life are *also* the years when they are most *financially* hindered by the unknowns of longevity and volatility risk."

Michael shook his head. "It's just so inefficient."

"That's right. When you make tiny withdrawals, there is a good chance that you will not run out of money. But you won't realize that until the *end* of your life, when you are *least* physically active. In those early years, when you are *most* able to be physically active, you are *least* able to be financially active. By the time you know whether or not your retirement has worked, you may not be able to use it in the way that you thought."

The years that retirees are most *physically* able to get out and experience life are *also* the years when they are most *financially* handicapped by the unknowns of longevity and volatility risk.

"It's just so inefficient," Michael said again.

"You nailed it," his father said. "The problem is that while saving more money and lowering the withdrawal rate will increase the chances of retirement success, it doesn't really solve the problem. Most of us can't save more money, and the income is not enough if we lower the withdrawal rate. Even a person like Sally—whose account is growing— doesn't know that from year to year. *We* have the benefit of hindsight. *We* can look at Sally's experience and say, 'Heck, she should have taken out more! She left a lot of money on the table!'" But Sally had no way of knowing that at the time, so she had to be careful. A random downturn here or there could change everything. What we need is a strategy that addresses the *real* problem."

"Okay," Michael said.

Kathleen smiled. "You're not getting off that easy. You need to tell *us* what you see as the problem with this chart."

Kathleen picked up the sheet of paper showing Sam retiring with $1 million and withdrawing $100,000 a year. She slid it under Michael's nose.

Michael grinned at the old family tradition. *I have to figure it out for myself.* He took a sip of coffee and looked at the chart.

"Well, I now know that actual returns produce *drastically* different results from average returns. So I would say the real problem with this chart is that, at times, a retiree is forced to sell investments in a down year. Mortgages still need to be paid, and, as my brilliant sister said, there is no *faster* way to run out of money than selling investments in a down year. And I guess this is *especially* true if those down years come at the beginning of a retirement."

> ## There is no *faster* way to run out of money than selling investments in a down year.

"I'd say you're right on, son," Edward said.

Michael picked up the sheet in front of him. His eyes zeroed in on the first few years of this hypothetical retirement.

The dangers of withdrawing income during negative years

Retirement Year	Actual Year	Beginning Year Balance	Withdrawal	Post Withdrawal Balance	S&P Return	End of Year Balance
1	1972	$1,000,000.00	$100,000.00	$900,000.00	19.15%	$1,072,350.00
2	1973	$1,072,350.00	$100,000.00	$972,350.00	-15.03%	$826,205.80
3	1974	$826,205.80	$100,000.00	$726,205.80	-26.95%	$530,493.33
4	1975	$530,493.33	$100,000.00	$430,493.33	38.46%	$596,061.07
5	1976	$596,061.07	$100,000.00	$496,061.07	24.20%	$616,107.85

Figure 9.3

An idea suddenly occurred to him.

"It would be nice if you didn't *have* to sell in a down year. Especially those down years that occur early on in retirement."

"Ahh!" Edward smiled. "That is *exactly* what this next strategy is about. Sam needs to Beat the Bear."

Michael gave his father a puzzled look. "Beat the Bear?"

"Yep. If Sam can beat off those bear-market years—especially during the early retirement years—then Sam would increase his chances of not running out of money."

"How is that possible?"

"It's possible when we move away from traditional B.S. retirement thinking and into the realm of efficiency planning," Edward went on. "It's not just how much you save, it's *how* you save it. When we try to save a lot of money, our goal is to get a big balance sheet. But that's not the problem we need to solve in retirement. In retirement, the real problem isn't lack of money, it's lack of *income*."

In retirement, the real problem isn't lack of money, it's lack of *income*.

"What if Sam had a reserve account—a Beat the Bear account—that he could pull from in the early years of his retirement? What if he didn't *have* to touch his market account in the early years? What if this Beat the Bear account was totally separate from the markets and was his defense against market downturns? What if we did not exacerbate a market loss with an income withdrawal?"

Edward let his son process this question for a moment. Then he slid another chart across the table.

Michael stared down at the chart, and several things hit him at once. The chart was largely similar, but he noticed that Sam was now withdrawing from two *separate* accounts, depending on the retirement year. In the years when the market was up, he would sell off his balance-sheet investments to create income. But in those early retirement years when the market was negative, Sam didn't sell. Instead, he took money out of his Beat the Bear account. This account protected the balance-sheet investments in his market account from being tapped in a down year.

1972-2001 with three years of
Beat the Bear bucks (not taking withdrawals)

Retirement Year	Actual Year	Beginning Year Balance	Withdrawal	Post Withdrawal Balance	S&P Return	End of Year Balance	Beat the Bear Account
1	1972	$1,000,000.00	$100,000.00	$900,000.00	19.15%	$1,072,350.00	
2	1973	$1,072,350.00	$-	$1,072,350.00	-15.03%	$911,175.80	$75,000.00
3	1974	$911,175.80	$-	$911,175.80	-26.95%	$665,613.92	$75,000.00
4	1975	$665,613.92	$100,000.00	$565,613.92	38.46%	$783,149.03	
5	1976	$783,149.03	$100,000.00	$683,149.03	24.20%	$848,471.10	
6	1977	$848,471.10	$-	$848,471.10	-7.78%	$782,460.05	$75,000.00
7	1978	$782,460.05	$100,000.00	$682,460.05	6.41%	$726,205.73	
8	1979	$726,205.73	$100,000.00	$626,205.73	18.69%	$743,243.59	
9	1980	$743,243.59	$100,000.00	$643,243.59	32.67%	$853,391.27	
10	1981	$853,391.27	$100,000.00	$753,391.27	-5.33%	$713,235.51	
11	1982	$713,235.51	$100,000.00	$613,235.51	21.22%	$743,364.09	
12	1983	$743,364.09	$100,000.00	$643,364.09	23.13%	$792,174.20	
13	1984	$792,174.20	$100,000.00	$692,174.20	5.96%	$733,427.78	
14	1985	$733,427.78	$100,000.00	$633,427.78	32.24%	$837,644.90	
15	1986	$837,644.90	$100,000.00	$737,644.90	19.06%	$878,240.02	
16	1987	$878,240.02	$100,000.00	$778,240.02	5.69%	$822,521.87	
17	1988	$822,521.87	$100,000.00	$722,521.87	16.64%	$842,749.51	
18	1989	$842,749.51	$100,000.00	$742,749.51	32.00%	$980,429.36	
19	1990	$980,429.36	$100,000.00	$880,429.36	-3.42%	$850,318.67	
20	1991	$850,318.67	$100,000.00	$750,318.67	30.95%	$982,542.30	
21	1992	$982,542.30	$100,000.00	$882,542.30	7.60%	$949,615.52	
22	1993	$949,615.52	$100,000.00	$849,615.52	10.17%	$936,021.42	
23	1994	$936,021.42	$100,000.00	$836,021.42	1.19%	$845,970.07	
24	1995	$845,970.07	$100,000.00	$745,970.07	38.02%	$1,029,587.89	
25	1996	$1,029,587.89	$100,000.00	$929,587.89	23.06%	$1,143,950.86	
26	1997	$1,143,950.86	$100,000.00	$1,043,950.86	33.67%	$1,395,449.12	
27	1998	$1,395,449.12	$100,000.00	$1,295,449.12	28.73%	$1,667,631.65	
28	1999	$1,667,631.65	$100,000.00	$1,567,631.65	21.11%	$1,898,558.69	
29	2000	$1,898,558.69	$100,000.00	$1,798,558.69	-9.11%	$1,634,709.99	
30	2001	$1,634,709.99	$100,000.00	$1,534,709.99	-11.98%	$1,350,851.74	
			Average Rate of Return		13.68%		

Figure 9.4

Edward let his son absorb the chart.

Michael realized that what the chart *really* showed is that while more money and lower withdrawals always help, the *real* issue is efficiency. People don't necessarily need to save more, they just need to have a more efficient plan. He realized that when a person saves some money in a different account, one that is free from the volatility of the markets, they can substantially reduce their exposure to volatility risk.

"See how much better the Beat the Bear strategy does against systematic withdrawal for the same period?" Edward placed the chart of returns from 1972 to 2001 side by side with the Beat the Bear chart from that same period. Michael saw that by having just a few years of income in a separate account, Sam was able to leave more than $1.3 million to his children, as opposed to running out of money in the 13th year of his retirement.

He took another moment to study the charts.

"So, the Beat the Bear account is kind of like a retirement emergency fund for when things don't go as planned," he finally said.

> ## The Beat the Bear account is kind of like a retirement emergency fund for when things don't go as planned.

"I'd say that's a great summary," Edward said. "The key idea to remember is that our Beat the Bear account should not be in the markets. We have to remember that the stock, bond, *and* real estate markets *all* took a hit in 2008."[1]

Edward knew that was true from his own experience. He himself had retired around that time. And he knew that one important revelation of the 2008 crash was that risk-based assets—stocks, bonds, and real estate— were now much more correlated than the financial planning industry originally thought. Most people *believe* they are properly diversified, but all too often, *all* their eggs are in the same basket—the *risk* basket.[2]

1972–2001 with three years of Beat the Bear bucks

Retirement Year	Actual Year	Beginning Year Balance	Withdrawal	Post Withdrawal Balance	S&P Return	End of Year Balance	Beat the Bear Account
1	1972	$1,000,000.00	$100,000.00	$900,000.00	19.15%	$1,072,350.00	
2	1973	$1,072,350.00	$-	$1,072,350.00	-15.03%	$911,175.80	$75,000.00
3	1974	$911,175.80	$-	$911,175.80	-26.95%	$665,613.92	$75,000.00
4	1975	$665,613.92	$100,000.00	$565,613.92	38.46%	$783,149.03	
5	1976	$783,149.03	$100,000.00	$683,149.03	24.20%	$848,471.10	
6	1977	$848,471.10	$-	$848,471.10	-7.78%	$782,460.05	$75,000.00
7	1978	$782,460.05	$100,000.00	$682,460.05	6.41%	$726,205.73	
8	1979	$726,205.73	$100,000.00	$626,205.73	18.69%	$743,243.59	
9	1980	$743,243.59	$100,000.00	$643,243.59	32.67%	$853,391.27	
10	1981	$853,391.27	$100,000.00	$753,391.27	-5.33%	$713,235.51	
11	1982	$713,235.51	$100,000.00	$613,235.51	21.22%	$743,364.09	
12	1983	$743,364.09	$100,000.00	$643,364.09	23.13%	$792,174.20	
13	1984	$792,174.20	$100,000.00	$692,174.20	5.96%	$733,427.78	
14	1985	$733,427.78	$100,000.00	$633,427.78	32.24%	$837,644.90	
15	1986	$837,644.90	$100,000.00	$737,644.90	19.06%	$878,240.02	
16	1987	$878,240.02	$100,000.00	$778,240.02	5.69%	$822,521.87	
17	1988	$822,521.87	$100,000.00	$722,521.87	16.64%	$842,749.51	
18	1989	$842,749.51	$100,000.00	$742,749.51	32.00%	$980,429.36	
19	1990	$980,429.36	$100,000.00	$880,429.36	-3.42%	$850,318.67	
20	1991	$850,318.67	$100,000.00	$750,318.67	30.95%	$982,542.30	
21	1992	$982,542.30	$100,000.00	$882,542.30	7.60%	$949,615.52	
22	1993	$949,615.52	$100,000.00	$849,615.52	10.17%	$936,021.42	
23	1994	$936,021.42	$100,000.00	$836,021.42	1.19%	$845,970.07	
24	1995	$845,970.07	$100,000.00	$745,970.07	38.02%	$1,029,587.89	
25	1996	$1,029,587.89	$100,000.00	$929,587.89	23.06%	$1,143,950.86	
26	1997	$1,143,950.86	$100,000.00	$1,043,950.86	33.67%	$1,395,449.12	
27	1998	$1,395,449.12	$100,000.00	$1,295,449.12	28.73%	$1,667,631.65	
28	1999	$1,667,631.65	$100,000.00	$1,567,631.65	21.11%	$1,898,558.69	
29	2000	$1,898,558.69	$100,000.00	$1,798,558.69	-9.11%	$1,634,709.99	
30	2001	$1,634,709.99	$100,000.00	$1,534,709.99	-11.98%	$1,350,851.74	
			Average Rate of Return		13.68%		

Vs. no Beat the Bear bucks

Retirement Year	Actual Year	Beginning Year Balance	Withdrawal	Post Withdrawal Balance	S&P Return	End of Year Balance
1	1972	$1,000,000.00	$100,000.00	$900,000.00	19.15%	$1,072,350.00
2	1973	$1,072,350.00	$100,000.00	$972,350.00	**-15.03%**	$826,205.80
3	1974	$826,205.80	$100,000.00	$726,205.80	**-26.95%**	$530,493.33
4	1975	$530,493.33	$100,000.00	$430,493.33	38.46%	$596,061.07
5	1976	$596,061.07	$100,000.00	$496,061.07	24.20%	$616,107.85
6	1977	$616,107.85	$100,000.00	$516,107.85	**-7.78%**	$475,954.66
7	1978	$475,954.66	$100,000.00	$375,954.66	6.41%	$400,053.35
8	1979	$400,053.35	$100,000.00	$300,053.35	**18.69%**	$356,133.32
9	1980	$356,133.32	$100,000.00	$256,133.32	32.67%	$339,812.08
10	1981	$339,812.08	$100,000.00	$239,812.08	**-5.33%**	$227,030.09
11	1982	$227,030.09	$100,000.00	$127,030.09	21.22%	$153,985.88
12	1983	$153,985.88	$100,000.00	$53,985.88	23.13%	$66,472.82
13	1984	$66,472.82	$100,000.00	$0	5.96%	$0
14	1985	$0	$100,000.00	$0	32.24%	$0
15	1986	$0	$100,000.00	$0	19.06%	$0
16	1987	$0	$100,000.00	$0	5.69%	$0
17	1988	$0	$100,000.00	$0	16.64%	$0
18	1989	$0	$100,000.00	$0	32.00%	$0
19	1990	$0	$100,000.00	$0	**-3.42%**	$0
20	1991	$0	$100,000.00	$0	30.95%	$0
21	1992	$0	$100,000.00	$0	7.60%	$0
22	1993	$0	$100,000.00	$0	10.17%	$0
23	1994	$0	$100,000.00	$0	1.19%	$0
24	1995	$0	$100,000.00	$0	38.02%	$0
25	1996	$0	$100,000.00	$0	23.06%	$0
26	1997	$0	$100,000.00	$0	33.67%	$0
27	1998	$0	$100,000.00	$0	28.73%	$0
28	1999	$0	$100,000.00	$0	21.11%	$0
29	2000	$0	$100,000.00	$0	**-9.11%**	$0
30	2001	$0	$100,000.00	$0	**-11.98%**	$0
				Average Rate of Return	13.68%	

Figure 9.5

He knew the problem of *true* lack of diversity can lie silent for years. It appears that all is well in an investor's portfolio. When you are working, down years are merely an opportunity to pick up bargains. The real problem reveals its ugly head at retirement. Retirees *think* they are insulated against market risk, when the opposite is true. Just because they are diversified, does not mean they are buffered. Low risk is not the same as *no* risk.

"We cannot buffer risk with risk," Edward said. "I know it sounds obvious, but that is how it is typically done when a person has 100 percent of their money in the markets. To *truly* protect ourselves, we need assets that won't go down when the markets inevitably go down."

We cannot buffer risk with risk.

Michael nodded. The concept made sense. He picked up the sheet of paper and studied it closely.

Suddenly, something hit him.

"Hey, wait a minute." He looked up at his father. "In one example, Sam has $1 million in his market account and he runs out of money in the 13th year. But when he uses the Beat the Bear strategy, the chart shows he makes it." Michael raised a finger. "However, Sam's Beat the Bear account has 225,000 'extra' dollars. Where did those extra dollars magically come from?"

Edward smiled. "I was wondering when you would catch that. And I am proud that you did. More than a few of my clients overlooked it.

"Indeed, in one example, a retiree has more money overall. So let's make it fair."

He slid another chart across the table. "In one example, Sam has $1.25 million in his market account and in the other example he has $1 million in his market account and $225,000 in his Beat the Bear account. You can see which does better."

Sam with $1.225 million in market account

Retirement Year	Actual Year	Beginning Year Balance	Withdrawal	Post Withdrawal Balance	S&P Return	End of Year Balance
1	1972	$1,225,000.00	$100,000.00	$1,125,000.00	19.15%	$1,340,437.50
2	1973	$1,340,437.50	$100,000.00	$1,240,437.50	-15.03%	$1,053,999.74
3	1974	$1,053,999.74	$100,000.00	$953,999.74	-26.95%	$696,896.81
4	1975	$696,896.81	$100,000.00	$596,896.81	38.46%	$826,463.33
5	1976	$826,463.33	$100,000.00	$726,463.33	24.20%	$902,267.45
6	1977	$902,267.45	$100,000.00	$802,267.45	-7.78%	$739,851.04
7	1978	$739,851.04	$100,000.00	$639,851.04	6.41%	$680,865.50
8	1979	$680,865.50	$100,000.00	$580,865.50	18.69%	$689,429.26
9	1980	$689,429.26	$100,000.00	$589,429.26	32.67%	$781,995.80
10	1981	$781,995.80	$100,000.00	$681,995.80	-5.33%	$645,645.42
11	1982	$645,645.42	$100,000.00	$545,645.42	21.22%	$661,431.38
12	1983	$661,431.38	$100,000.00	$561,431.38	23.13%	$691,290.46
13	1984	$691,290.46	$100,000.00	$591,290.46	5.96%	$626,531.37
14	1985	$626,531.37	$100,000.00	$526,531.37	32.24%	$696,285.08
15	1986	$696,285.08	$100,000.00	$596,285.08	19.06%	$709,937.02
16	1987	$709,937.02	$100,000.00	$609,937.02	5.69%	$644,642.43
17	1988	$644,642.43	$100,000.00	$544,642.43	16.64%	$635,270.93
18	1989	$635,270.93	$100,000.00	$535,270.93	32.00%	$706,557.63
19	1990	$706,557.63	$100,000.00	$606,557.63	-3.42%	$585,813.36
20	1991	$585,813.36	$100,000.00	$485,813.36	30.95%	$636,172.60
21	1992	$636,172.60	$100,000.00	$536,172.60	7.60%	$576,921.71
22	1993	$576,921.71	$100,000.00	$476,921.71	10.17%	$525,424.65
23	1994	$525,424.65	$100,000.00	$425,424.65	1.19%	$430,487.20
24	1995	$430,487.20	$100,000.00	$330,487.20	38.02%	$456,138.44
25	1996	$456,138.44	$100,000.00	$356,138.44	23.06%	$438,263.96
26	1997	$438,263.96	$100,000.00	$338,263.96	33.67%	$452,157.44
27	1998	$452,157.44	$100,000.00	$352,157.44	28.73%	$453,332.27
28	1999	$453,332.27	$100,000.00	$353,332.27	21.11%	$427,920.72
29	2000	$427,920.72	$100,000.00	$327,920.72	-9.11%	$298,047.14
30	2001	$298,047.14	$100,000.00	$198,047.14	-11.98%	$174,321.09
				Average Rate of Return	13.68%	

Sam with $1 million in his market account and
$225,000 in his Beat the Bear account

Retirement Year	Actual Year	Beginning Year Balance	Withdrawal	Post Withdrawal Balance	S&P Return	End of Year Balance	Beat the Bear Account
1	1972	$1,000,000.00	$100,000.00	$900,000.00	19.15%	$1,072,350.00	
2	1973	$1,072,350.00	$-	$1,072,350.00	-15.03%	$911,175.80	$75,000.00
3	1974	$911,175.80	$-	$911,175.80	-26.95%	$665,613.92	$75,000.00
4	1975	$665,613.92	$100,000.00	$565,613.92	38.46%	$783,149.03	
5	1976	$783,149.03	$100,000.00	$683,149.03	24.20%	$848,471.10	
6	1977	$848,471.10	$-	$848,471.10	-7.78%	$782,460.05	$75,000.00
7	1978	$782,460.05	$100,000.00	$682,460.05	6.41%	$726,205.73	
8	1979	$726,205.73	$100,000.00	$626,205.73	18.69%	$743,243.59	
9	1980	$743,243.59	$100,000.00	$643,243.59	32.67%	$853,391.27	
10	1981	$853,391.27	$100,000.00	$753,391.27	-5.33%	$713,235.51	
11	1982	$713,235.51	$100,000.00	$613,235.51	21.22%	$743,364.09	
12	1983	$743,364.09	$100,000.00	$643,364.09	23.13%	$792,174.20	
13	1984	$792,174.20	$100,000.00	$692,174.20	5.96%	$733,427.78	
14	1985	$733,427.78	$100,000.00	$633,427.78	32.24%	$837,644.90	
15	1986	$837,644.90	$100,000.00	$737,644.90	19.06%	$878,240.02	
16	1987	$878,240.02	$100,000.00	$778,240.02	5.69%	$822,521.87	
17	1988	$822,521.87	$100,000.00	$722,521.87	16.64%	$842,749.51	
18	1989	$842,749.51	$100,000.00	$742,749.51	32.00%	$980,429.36	
19	1990	$980,429.36	$100,000.00	$880,429.36	-3.42%	$850,318.67	
20	1991	$850,318.67	$100,000.00	$750,318.67	30.95%	$982,542.30	
21	1992	$982,542.30	$100,000.00	$882,542.30	7.60%	$949,615.52	
22	1993	$949,615.52	$100,000.00	$849,615.52	10.17%	$936,021.42	
23	1994	$936,021.42	$100,000.00	$836,021.42	1.19%	$845,970.07	
24	1995	$845,970.07	$100,000.00	$745,970.07	38.02%	$1,029,587.89	
25	1996	$1,029,587.89	$100,000.00	$929,587.89	23.06%	$1,143,950.86	
26	1997	$1,143,950.86	$100,000.00	$1,043,950.86	33.67%	$1,395,449.12	
27	1998	$1,395,449.12	$100,000.00	$1,295,449.12	28.73%	$1,667,631.65	
28	1999	$1,667,631.65	$100,000.00	$1,567,631.65	21.11%	$1,898,558.69	
29	2000	$1,898,558.69	$100,000.00	$1,798,558.69	-9.11%	$1,634,709.99	
30	2001	$1,634,709.99	$100,000.00	$1,534,709.99	-11.98%	$1,350,851.74	
			Average Rate of Return		13.68%		$225,000

Figure 9.6

Michael studied the charts. He saw that in the example with $1.225 million in the market, Sam made it all the way through retirement, but died with just under $175,000. In the other example, with the *same* amount of money but with some of it allocated in a separate, nonmarket account, Sam passed away leaving more than $1.3 *million* to his heirs.

"Whatdaya think?" Kathleen smiled.

"Well," Michael looked up at his sister. "I guess it's not just how much you save, it's *how* you save it."

It's not just how much you save, it's *how* you save it.

Edward slapped the table. "That's *exactly* it, son. More money alone won't cut it. The crash of 2008 taught us many things, but perhaps the most potent lesson is that so many market-based investments, like stocks, bonds, and real estate, are correlated *much* more than we realized. When we subject all our retirement dollars to the markets, we run the risk of them all going down at once. However, when we allocate some dollars outside the markets, we can protect ourselves from market downturns."

Michael nodded. The idea made sense. "I get it. Even though in both examples, Sam 'made it,' in one he was able to leave behind a healthy legacy, while in the other, in comparison, he had a minimal amount."

"That's not all, baby bro," Kathleen said. "Look at the last few years of the example with all the money in the markets. Yes, Sam did have money left over when he passed away. In *hindsight,* we know he made it. But think about what *actually* would be going through Sam's head in those final years. Look at year 23. The market only returned 1.19 percent. His retirement account *drops* by almost a quarter. The next year's gain of 38 percent helped a lot, but Sam would not know that at the *time.* Compare that to the example with the Beat the Bear account. Sam has nearly *double* that much money in year 23. Yes, the math on a spreadsheet is important to understand, but what can *never* be understood by looking at spreadsheets is the *emotional* stress a retiree is going through, not knowing what the markets will do next year."

Michael let his sister's words sink in. She was right. It was one thing to stare at pieces of paper with hindsight data. It was another thing to *live* it.

"Okay," he finally said. "But why did we only pull $75,000 from our Beat the Bear account? I mean, wasn't our target income $100,000?"

"It was," Edward said. "But remember, it's not what you make, it's what you keep. When a person pulls money out of their 401(k), 403(b), or traditional IRA, that income is *taxable*. So $100,000 in withdrawals might result in $75,000 in income after taxes."

"Fair enough," Michael nodded.

"Well, what if there was an account where withdrawals could be done tax-*free*? Then, the tax-free withdrawal of $75,000 would be equivalent to a *taxable* withdrawal of $100,000. Remember, you don't need more money, you need more *income*."[3]

"Okay," Michael said. "What account gets that?"

Michael's Notebook:

- When using the systematic withdrawal strategy, the only way to protect against longevity risk and sequence-of-return risk is to lower the withdrawal rate.
  ◊ More money can help, but it doesn't necessarily guarantee success.
  ◊ Lowering the withdrawal rate below 4 percent can help, but this is *extremely inefficient!*
- It's very dangerous to sell investments in a down year, *especially* during early retirement years.
- Instead, create a Beat the Bear account.
  ◊ This is totally separate from the markets. (You cannot buffer risk with risk!)
  ◊ Pull from this account when markets are down, and leave $$$ in market accounts alone.
  ◊ With the same money, you can have *more* income! (It's all about efficiency!)
- Where is best place for a Beat the Bear account?

CHAPTER 10

ADDING OXYGEN

E dward downed his coffee and stood up.

"That barn is not going to paint itself. Let's talk while we work. Why don't you help your ninja sister?"

Within 10 minutes Kathleen was up on the ladder, swinging her paintbrush back and forth. Michael took his position midway on the shorter ladder. His father moved to an unpainted section of the wall and painted the words: *Beat the Bear*. "Let's think of some of the characteristics of this account. What would we like to see it have?"

"Well, obviously no risk of loss," Michael said. "But it should get *some* growth. At least match or beat what the banks are paying."

"I like that," Edward said.

"Tax-favored always works for me," Kathleen yelled.

Michael glanced up at his sister. "Tax-favored? What gets that?"

But before she could answer, his father jumped in. "I'll add my favorite," Edward said. "How about if you die, some or all of the funds you used up during your retirement get replenished and sent to your spouse or kids?"

Michael looked at his father and smiled. Then he craned his head and looked at his father's artwork.

BEAT THE BEAR

No risk of loss

Modest growth

Tax-favored

Funds replenished upon death

What account gets all that? Michael thought. Then he got it.

"Gee, Dad, this sounds a lot like life insurance."

"That's right," Edward grinned. He moved away from his artwork on the barn wall. "When we look for the best place to build our beat the bear account, permanent life insurance wins out."

Michael shook his head. "I don't know. Our whole-life policies are expensive. I'm thinking Jill and I should cancel them and buy term policies. Then we can invest the difference. Our advisor agrees."

Edward smiled to himself. Buying term and investing the rest in the markets was just more B.S. thinking. But he knew most people thought like his son. Michael was quoting the advice of the TV gurus and financial authors who never highlighted the benefits of permanent life, or whole-life, insurance. Many experts viewed permanent life insurance merely as an apples-to-apples competitor with term insurance, without realizing the product can be used in many different ways. Those same experts taught people how to get *to* retirement but failed to discuss how to get *through* retirement.

"That's a popular idea," Edward said. "But let me ask you two questions. You say your advisor is adamant about you not buying whole-life insurance. How long have you been with this advisor?"

"Jill and I have been with him for eight years."

"And in those eight years, did your advisor ever once mention safe withdrawal rates?"

"Aside from our last meeting, no."

"And that was the meeting that brought you here?"

"Yeah. Up until that meeting, the focus was always reviewing how much our nest egg had grown and how to make it grow bigger."

"And that's very common," Edward said. "Most financial advisors are very good at helping you build up a big pile of money in the markets. Every year your brokerage account gets bigger and bigger. When you see how much it grows, why would you *ever* think about a whole-life insurance policy? That would just be allocating dollars *away* from all this explosive growth.

> ## Most financial advisors are very good at helping you build up a big pile of money in the markets.

"But as we have seen, more money alone won't solve the problem. Don't fall into the B.S. trap, because that's not the answer. *Efficiency* is the answer. And life insurance can help with that."

"How?" Michael said.

"Well, first we need to remember that whole-life insurance is really just one type of *permanent* insurance. Permanent insurance, as you know, is any insurance that lasts for your entire lifetime. Term insurance is any insurance that lasts for a certain *term*, say 20 or 30 years. If the term policyholder dies during the term, the policy pays out. If the person dies one day after the term runs out, there is no payout."

Michael nodded. "I know. You spent your 'whole life helping people learn about whole life.' Permanent insurance is just life insurance that lasts for as long as a person lives."

"But it's more than just life insurance," Kathleen said. "Remember part of the premiums on a permanent insurance policy go into an account that builds up a cash value. The earnings on this account are not correlated to any of the markets. And, over time, those earnings are typically higher than what a bank savings account is paying. What's more, the earnings in a permanent life insurance policy are tax-favored."

"So that cash value is the best place for the Beat the Bear account?" Michael asked.

"In most cases, yes," Edward said. "When a person purchases a permanent life insurance policy in their 30s, 40s, or 50s, they are giving the cash-value portion of the policy time to grow. By the time they reach retirement, that cash account is large enough to Beat the Bear. Rather than pull money out of their market accounts, a person would pull from their Beat the Bear account.

"Remember our two scenarios with Sam's retirement? In one example, he saved $1.225 million dollars in the *market*. In the other scenario, he saved only $1 million in the markets and $225,000 in his Beat the Bear account."

Michael nodded.

"Well, his Beat the Bear account was actually a permanent life insurance policy. The policy might not grow as fast as the markets, but it didn't *need* to. By being *separate* from the markets, he was able to make his retirement income last. That is what the Fifth Option is all about. By moving *away* from the safe withdrawal strategy, he got a better retirement outcome."

"And that's not all, baby bro," Kathleen yelled from above. "When he died, the life insurance policy paid out any remaining death benefit to his spouse. Think about that. His spouse would get an injection of cash at some point in her retirement. That wouldn't happen if he had saved the money in a bank account."

"Your sister's right," Edward said. "And if Sam and his wife passed away at the same time, or within a few years of each other, their life insurance policies would leave a nice legacy for the kids."

"Here's how I look at it," Kathleen said. "I like to think of balance-sheet investments as the hydrogen in a portfolio. Hydrogen is the lightest element, and it is highly explosive. It has the ability to do great things, to earn great returns. But it can also blow up in an investor's face. It's happened in the past, and it will happen again."

"Many investors have financial amnesia," Edward added. "But market downturns are a fact of life. Investors are all too quick to forget 2008, 2001, 1990, and 1987. And those are just the *recent* ones."

"Markets go up *and* down," Kathleen continued. "A crash *will* happen, and a recovery *will* happen, and the cycle will happen again. It's just impossible to predict exactly *when* it will happen. That is why a hydrogen portfolio needs some oxygen to complement it."

"Everyone knows that oxygen is necessary to sustain life, but few people know that oxygen is *not* flammable. On its own, it does not burn. What oxygen does is allow other elements to ignite at a lower temperature and burn hotter. It helps other fuels burn better."

"I did not know that," Michael smiled. "I never knew you were an amateur chemist."

"One of my many talents," Kathleen smiled back. She dragged her paintbrush in a long, smooth line. "But think about it. Rockets are powered by a mixture of hydrogen *and* oxygen. Without both, there is no liftoff. Or think of a blacksmith's bellows. When blacksmiths pump their bellows, they are pumping oxygen into the forge to make it hotter."

"I bet I know what you are going to say next, Kath. Oxygen is the life insurance policy."

"Ya got me," Kathleen said. "Oxygen does not burn; *it only helps other things burn better.* Our life insurance account cannot do the work on its own; it is not a replacement for hydrogen and it cannot do what hydrogen can do. It is there to *help* our hydrogen account burn hotter."

"I love this example," Edward said. "It reminds us that we need to step away from the either-or mentality. It's not either investments *or* insurance. It's investments *and* insurance. Just think, what happens when we put hydrogen and oxygen together? What do we get?"

We need to step away from the either-or mentality. It's not either investments *or* insurance. It's investments *and* insurance.

"H2O," Michael said. "Water, the building block of life."

"And the building block of the Beat the Bear Strategy," Edward said. "Now retirees will have different mixtures, but the concept is the same. We need *both* hydrogen and oxygen. That's what gets us to and *through* retirement. Most people already have the hydrogen component; they just need to add oxygen."

"Like salt and pepper," Michael said.

"Or Fred and Ginger," Kathleen said.

"Pick whatever analogy you like, but, yes," Edward said. "In the past, most people had the right mixture already made for them. That mixture was called a pension."

Michael made a few strokes with his paintbrush as he let the Beat the Bear Strategy sink in for a moment. Slowly, he was starting to rethink his view on those whole-life insurance policies.

"I like this strategy," he finally said. "I feel I have a pretty good handle on my investments and want them to be part of my retirement, and I enjoy researching them. The Beat the Bear Strategy allows me to still have a hand in my investments without *forcing* my hand to sell during retirement. I get it. It will smooth out what might be bumpy rides in the markets."

"I'd say that's a perfect summary," Edward said. "Your sister, however, had a different take."

Michael looked up at his sister on the ladder.

"Whatcha thinking?"

"When Dad explained this strategy to me, I saw the importance of Beating the Bear markets at the beginning," she said. "Those early retirement years are very fragile, and it's important to have a nonmarket account to pull from. But I am the *opposite* of you, brother . . . I do not want my investments to be the focus, and I do not like to do all of the research and monitor them like you do."

"Go on."

"And the Beat the Bear Strategy is still not *guaranteed*," she said. "You still *could* run out of money. What if Sam retired at a time when he needed *five* years of Beat the Bear bucks? It could happen. Increasing the amount of Beat the Bear bucks helps increase the chances for success, but it does not *guarantee* it. The strategy is still heavily dependent on turning market assets into cash for income. The life insurance is just there as a buffer, so we don't have to sell in a down year. So it's a great strategy for people who are okay with watching their stock accounts for 30 years or more, for those people who want a chance at that upside. But for me, I wanted a smoother ride."

"So, what else can you do?"

"Remember the Desert Island Problem?" Edward asked.

"Sure," Michael said. "We don't know how long we will live, and we don't know what the market will do. So we are forced to take small sips, no matter how big our retirement barrel is."

"Well, one way to solve the Desert Island Problem," Edward tapped his container of paint, "is with buckets."

Michael's Notebook:

- A Beat the Bear account should have:
  - ◊ No risk of loss
  - ◊ Tax-favored status
  - ◊ Modest growth
  - ◊ A way to replenish itself upon death
- Permanent (whole) life insurance meets all these requirements.
- It has a cash account that grows tax-free with guaranteed growth.
- It has no exposure to market risk.
  - ◊ Hydrogen in portfolio = markets (great for growth but can be explosive).
  - ◊ Oxygen in portfolio = insurance (helps the hydrogen—markets— burn hotter).
  - ◊ It's *not* an either-or equation. It's *not* markets *or* insurance. It's markets *and* insurance.
- This strategy is still heavily dependent on the markets.
  - ◊ A retiree needs to sell gains to generate income.
  - ◊ A life insurance account is just a buffer.
- Great strategy for people who don't mind monitoring their investments.
- What about those who want a more hands-off approach?
- Buckets???

CHAPTER 11

THE BUCKET STRATEGY

"Buckets?" Michael asked. "I've heard of something called the Bucket Strategy, but I'm not sure how it works."

"The Bucket Strategy is the second strategy in the Fifth Option war chest," said Edward. "While the Beat the Bear Strategy is great for taking full advantage of the market's upside, it still relies on the market for generating income. A Beat the Bear account is only there as an emergency fund for a limited number of down years.

"But the Bucket Strategy differs because it introduces three important retirement planning concepts," he went on. "The first is the importance of establishing a preservation phase to our retirement plan. Most people see their financial lives in two phases: an accumulation phase and a distribution phase. The accumulation phase consists of our working years, when we are trying to save as much money as possible. The distribution phase encompasses our retirement years, when we are taking money *out* of our retirement accounts."

"Makes sense," Michael said.

"But the Bucket Strategy incorporates a middle stage, the preservation phase," Edward said. "This is a rolling 10-year block of time that protects us from volatility throughout our golden years but is *especially* important around our actual retirement date. Though this 10-year preservation phase keeps rolling all through our retirement, it's the years right before and right after our retirement date that are the most sensitive to market volatility.[1]

"These years have the biggest impact on whether we will have the retirement we want or not."

Edward drew a crude diagram on the side of the barn.

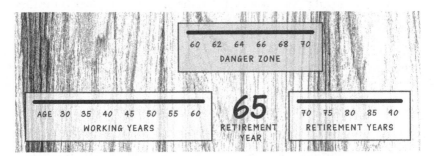

Figure 11.1

"We already saw the devastating impact that negative market returns can have on your retirement, *especially* during those early years. That 10-year block—the five years before you retire and the five years right after you retire—is *the* most susceptible to sequence-of-return risk. I like to call that time period the retirement danger zone. How you manage your money during the retirement danger zone can make or break your retirement. Make the wrong decision and you might not recover.

> That 10-year block—the five years
> before you retire and the five years
> right after you retire—is *the* most
> susceptible to sequence-of-return risk.

"We saw from the Beat the Bear Strategy that having just a few years of income in a separate, nonmarket account can go a long way toward ensuring we don't run out of money. The Bucket Strategy takes this idea one step further. By establishing a rolling 10-year preservation phase," Edward continued, "we create a decade of predictable and sometimes even *guaranteed* income."

"In other words, 10 years of peace of mind," Kathleen said.

Edward turned toward Michael. "So the preservation phase is the first concept highlighted by the Bucket Strategy. The second concept is the idea of separating our money into, well, buckets. Each bucket is assigned a job and a time line to complete that job. That way we can increase the efficiency of our retirement dollars." He noticed Michael nodding along as he spoke, but he wasn't sure his son was comprehending the words.

"Let's back up to the Beat the Bear Strategy, so you can see the difference," Edward said. "In a sense, every retirement strategy outside of the systematic withdrawal strategy is a form of a Bucket Strategy. You can think of the Beat the Bear as a two-bucket strategy: One bucket has our market investments. Let's call that our risk bucket. Then we have another bucket that has our nonrisk investments—the cash value of our life insurance policy. Let's call that our nonrisk bucket. By having a few years of income in our nonrisk bucket, it's possible to safely increase the withdrawal rate."

"Okay, so how is the Bucket Strategy different than Beat the Bear?"

"That brings us to the third concept. The Bucket Strategy does not use the markets as your primary source of income. With the Beat the Bear Strategy, the markets *are* the primary source of your income. Every year, we will sell some of our market investments to generate the cash we need. The nonrisk bucket is only there for the few random years when we might need it—when the market is negative. Beat the Bear is a great strategy for people who are comfortable with the ups and downs of the markets. By having the majority of your portfolio in the markets, you can enjoy the aggressive growth the markets are known to provide. In short, you have a chance at a bigger upside."

The Bucket Strategy does not use the markets as your primary source of income.

Edward raised his paintbrush like a warning finger. "But the key thing to remember with Beat the Bear is that we are asking the dollars in our market account—the risk bucket—to perform *two* jobs: to provide our income *and* to provide growth.

"What's more, the Beat the Bear Strategy does not assign any time lines for accessing any of our dollars. Think about a traditional investment portfolio during the accumulation phase. In this phase, we have the luxury of having a long-term horizon. We put money into our retirement accounts knowing we will not be tapping into that account for many years. This is a great strategy, since markets tend to do well over time.

"But in retirement, we need our dollars to *both* last a long time *and* provide us annual income. Some dollars we need right away for income, while other dollars we won't need for many years. With Beat the Bear, most of our dollars are in the market, which is great for the long term but not always great in the short term.

"The Bucket Strategy recognizes this problem and makes a slight, but powerful, change: We no longer rely on the markets as our primary source of income. The dollars that we need to produce income have already been segregated from our risk bucket. With the Bucket Strategy, we will never ask the same dollar to do two jobs. And every dollar will have a specific time line to do that job."

"How so?"

The Bucket Strategy divides your retirement money into three buckets. Each bucket has a job and a time line to do that job.

"The Bucket Strategy divides your retirement money into three buckets. Each bucket has a job and a time line to do that job."

Edward moved over to an unpainted area of the barn. "I better talk fast. I am running out of room."

Michael watched as his father painted three crude buckets on the side of the barn.

"The first bucket is called the Now Bucket. Its job is to take care of anything that needs to be paid within the year. So, the Now Bucket would take care of our everyday needs and contain our emergency fund."

Edward took a smaller brush and wrote some words inside the first bucket. What he drew looked something like this[2]:

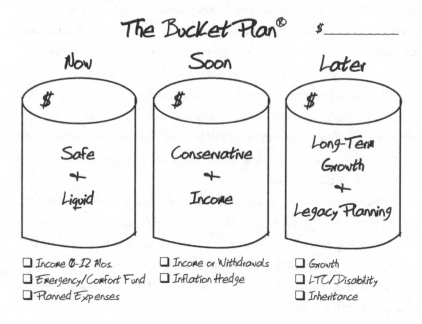

Figure 11.2

"So that money has to be super safe," Michael said. "Like a bank account?"

"Exactly. This is money you may need to draw on *tomorrow*, so it cannot have any risk. It must be 100 percent liquid."

Edward painted as he spoke. "The next bucket is our Soon Bucket. The Soon Bucket's job is to provide *income* for the next 10 years. Think of the Soon Bucket as our rolling preservation phase.

"And the final bucket is the Later Bucket. Its *only* job is to provide growth."

Edward finished writing in the words.

"Okay," Michael said. "I get the Now Bucket. Tell me more about the Soon and Later Buckets."

"The theory is pretty simple," Edward said. "We know the fastest way to run out of money in retirement is to sell investments during down markets. With the Beat the Bear Strategy, we saw how powerful it was to have a separate account *outside* of the markets to pull money from in a market down year."

"Sure," Michael said. "Our oxygen account helps the hydrogen account burn hotter."

"Exactly," Edward said. "The Bucket Strategy just extends this concept of separating accounts. What we want is for each of the buckets to have the right instruments for the right job and the right time frame to complete them. Some financial vehicles are great for generating income, but they are terrible at generating growth. Other financial vehicles are great for generating growth, but they do not convert easily into income."

"Einstein stated, 'You cannot simultaneously prevent and prepare for war,'" Kathleen yelled down to them. "Likewise, it's hard for the markets to efficiently grow *and* provide income. With the Bucket Strategy, we won't ask the *markets* to provide our income."

"Instead, our income will come from having a predictable 10-year income stream in our Soon Bucket," Edward said. "That prevents us from being forced to draw on the Later Bucket for up to 10 years. Over time, the markets tend to be the best growth option, but all that growth gets eroded when we sell investments in a down year. So we separate our dollars by not asking the *same* dollar to grow *and* provide income. We will *only* require the markets to do what they do best: grow.

"The Soon Bucket's job is to provide 10 years of predictable income," he went on. "Because the income is predictable, and sometimes even *guaranteed*, we have mitigated the sequence-of-return risk for up to 10 years. As the 10-year period ends, we refill the Soon Bucket with the market growth from the Later Bucket. When executed properly, retirees won't have to worry about next year's income. Retirees will always have at least a handful of years of income in their Soon Bucket. By segmenting our dollars, we can allow each bucket to focus solely on the job it does best."

"Okay, I understand the three buckets," Michael said. "I get that the Now Bucket has to be 100 percent safe and liquid. And I see that the Later Bucket is all about growth, so it makes sense the dollars in that bucket are in the markets. But what's in the Soon Bucket?"

"Depending on the economic environment at the time, the dollars in the Soon Bucket could be invested in a variety of financial vehicles," Edward said. "The key is that whatever those financial vehicles are, they must be low-risk to no-risk products with some modest income. As long as it provides the predictability we are looking for, there are possible choices in the banking, financial, and insurance world."

Michael examined the three buckets on the wall:

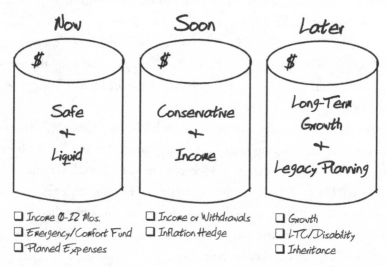

Figure 11.3

"So, the Now Bucket is our spending money. The Now Bucket is funded by the Soon Bucket, which is our income. We have 10 years of predictable income in the Soon Bucket. But when the Soon Bucket gets low, we replenish it with the growth from the Later Bucket."

"Wash. Rinse. Repeat," Edward said.

Michael thought about the strategy. It was simple but powerful. By not assigning multiple jobs to the same dollars, the dollars became more efficient at the one job they had. By segmenting money, a retiree didn't have all their eggs in one . . . bucket. He smiled at the joke.

Then he thought about his wife, the more conservative voice in their marriage. She would think the Bucket Strategy offered more predictability, but it still might not be enough.

"Whatcha thinkin'?" asked Edward.

"I'm thinking about what Jill would say. I can see how the Bucket Strategy reduces sequence-of-return and longevity risk. But it doesn't *guarantee* it."

"Jill's a smart woman. That is a concern. The Bucket Strategy *reduces* the risk of retirement failure, but it does not guarantee it. Even though we have extended our predictable income time period, we are still relying on the markets."

"And you need to keep managing those market dollars," Kathleen said.

Edward nodded. "Retirees would need to keep an eye on the Later Bucket. They might not sell *exactly* in year 10. They might sell some investments earlier, depending on how the markets are performing."

"But that's still market timing," Michael said. "I'm comfortable with a little of that, but my wife would prefer to have as little market timing as possible. She's looking for more of what her father's girlfriend has, a real pension. A retirement strategy that *guarantees* income, for *life*."

"Lots of people feel the way your wife does," Edward said. "Sadly they are not told about options outside of a B.S.-only strategy. But the good news is, what Jill wants is possible."

Michael brightened up. "Really?"

"Yes. There is only one way for a retiree who does not have a traditional pension to get guaranteed income for *life*."

Michael's Notebook:

The Bucket Strategy:

- Establishes three concepts:
  ◊ Concept #1—your retirement has three phases:
    — Accumulation phase = working years
    — Distribution phase = retirement years
    — Preservation phase = rolling 10-year period where 10 years of income is always safe
  ◊ Concept #2—this strategy assigns each bucket a job and a time line to do that job
    — Don't ask the same dollar to do two jobs. (It's difficult to allocate the same dollar to grow *and* create income.)
    — We can segment our money into buckets, each with specific jobs and time lines to increase the efficiency of every dollar we have.
  ◊ Concept #3—does not get income from selling market gains
    — With Beat the Bear, which has two buckets—risk (growth) and nonrisk (super safe)—retirees must sell their market gains to generate income.
    — The Bucket Strategy has a third bucket, the "Soon" Bucket, which provides the income.
- The 3 Buckets:
  ◊ Now Bucket:
    — 100 percent safe
    — Liquid
    — The job of the Now Bucket is to pay everyday bills and hold emergency funds.

◊ Soon Bucket:

  — This bucket earns predictable modest growth from banking, financial, and insurance products.

  — The job of the Soon Bucket is to provide 10 years of predictable income.

◊ Later Bucket:

  — The job of the Later Bucket is to grow market-based investments.

  — The Soon Bucket provides funds for the Now Bucket; as the Soon Bucket gets low on funds, we can replace those funds with dollars from the Later Bucket.

• But how do we get guaranteed income for life???

CHAPTER 12

JUMPING INTO THE POOL

"**G**uaranteed income for *life?*" Michael said.

"Absolutely," Edward said. "We've talked about two strategies so far that make income the primary focus. In the Beat the Bear Strategy, we accomplish that by having a separate, non-market account that we can draw on during down-market years. When we aren't forced to sell investments in a negative year, we can safely increase our withdrawal rate. With the Bucket Strategy, we are taking the separate account idea even further by having at least 10 years of income set aside. We are segmenting our dollars into *three* buckets, each with a specific job and a specific time line to do that job.

"But both of these strategies still depend on the market for growth and require some market monitoring. Some retirees won't want that. Instead, they'll want a strategy where they do not have to worry about the market's volatility at *all*. They'll let go of the chance for a bigger upside in exchange for the freedom to travel and do other things without the need to follow their investment through ups and downs. In fact, in my experience, the older we get, the more we fall into this camp! For these folks, this next strategy is for them. It might just be the strategy that creates the most predictable income of all."

"That would be me," Kathleen said. "I've never met Jill's father's girl-friend, but I want to be just like her when I retire. She was lucky enough to have a pension from her work. That's why she doesn't worry in her retirement. She knows how much she is going to get, and she knows she will receive it for the rest of her life. For her, longevity and volatility risk have all but disappeared."

"Yeah," Michael said. "I guess Doris has what retirees *really* want, which is not just the promise of more money but the guarantee of more *income*."

Michael smiled to himself. "Ya know, a day ago I would have said that sounds silly. I mean if you want more income you need to save more money, right? But that is B.S. thinking. I've seen firsthand that more money doesn't make the difference. If people are going to use the more money approach, they will need a *lot* more money."

"Sadly, that's how many people will try to solve their retirement income dilemma, by trying to save more money. They fail to realize that even with a bigger barrel, they still have to take small sips," Kathleen said.

"Okay, Dad, what's this third strategy?"

"The third strategy is all about creating a lifetime stream of guaranteed income."

"You mean like a pension but for an individual?"

"That's right, son. It *is* possible for *anyone* to have their own pension regardless of what their employer offers. But before I tell you how to create your own pension, it's important to know why pensions are such a power-ful retirement tool. Pensions are great for generating income because they have one significant advantage over an investment fund."

It *is* possible for *anyone* to have their own pension regardless of what their employer offers.

Michael cocked his head. "What's that?"

"A pension has two components," Edward explained. "The first component is the *investment* side. The funds for pensions are collected from employers or employees or from both. Then those funds are invested in any number of financial vehicles.

"But what separates a pension from a regular retirement account is the second component: the guaranteed income stream. Pensions make use of the second component, which allows investors to trade dollars for *guaranteed* income. And the way that a pension is able to deliver guaranteed income is by harnessing the power of actuarial science. Actuarial science is what opens up a whole new world of retirement-income possibilities."

"Actuarial science?" Michael said. "You mean guessing how long people will live?"

"That's right," his father said. "And it's definitely not guessing! Actuarial science attracts some brilliant minds in the mathematical field. While actuarial science takes many forms, for our purposes, the most basic explanation of actuarial science is simply that it's the science of determining how long a pool of people is going to live. It allows pension managers to determine payout rates. A pension without actuarial science is nothing more than an investment fund. But an investment fund that incorporates actuarial science suddenly *becomes* a pension.

"The idea of using actuarial science in financial planning is nothing new," Edward explained. "It's one of the oldest sciences, and it has an interesting history."

Michael made a long stroke with his paintbrush and smiled. He was starting to really enjoy his father's stories.

"Actuarial science goes all the way back to the Roman Empire," Edward said. "To be sure, the Romans didn't have the understanding that we have today. But they did realize they could spread out risk by creating risk *pools*. Some of the earliest uses of actuarial science involved people paying into communal funds for burial costs. The Romans didn't know who was going to die or when, they just knew that not everyone was going to die at the same time.

"In the 17th century many scholars were starting to dabble in actuarial science, including a theologian named Casper Neumann. He kept very accurate records on the deaths in his town of Breslau, which is now part of Poland.

"Neumann's data eventually found its way into the hands of Edmond Halley, the brilliant mathematician of Halley's Comet fame.

"It was Halley who showed how to set up an insurance system that could predict how much money should be collected as premiums. He also showed how much the insurance system could expect to pay out. It was the first public demonstration not just of what actuarial science could predict but also how it could be *used*.

"Edmond Halley could be considered a founding father of actuarial science because he eventually put his findings into print. He published a book with the Royal Society of London entitled *An Estimate of the Degrees of the Mortality of Mankind, Drawn from Curious Tables of the Births and Funerals at the City of Breslau, With an Attempt to Ascertain the Price of Annuities upon Lives*.

"Halley's book ended up being the financial and mathematical blueprint on how to create a pension. But what's important for us to realize is that actuarial science can help maximize retirement income streams." Edward turned to Michael and glanced up at Kathleen. "I think that's a great topic for lunch."

"I was hoping you would say that," Kathleen said.

* * *

Within 15 minutes, Michael, Kathleen, and Edward were seated at the picnic table and tucking into a plate of turkey sandwiches, a basket of potato chips, and a bowl filled with a colorful salad.

Michael caught sight of the familiar brown leather briefcase at his father's side. The three of them ate in silence for several minutes until Michael prodded his father to continue the conversation. "Okay, Dad, you were talking about how actuarial science can help with retirement income."

Edward finished chewing. "Let's use our desert island example again, only this time with real retirement solutions. Suppose you are 65 years old, you have saved $1 million in your retirement account, and the average life expectancy is 83. How long would you plan to make sure your money would last? To age 83, right?"

Michael took a bite and thought carefully. "Actually, no. We've had aunts and uncles who lived to their 90s."

"So, you would *not* create a retirement plan that spends your last dollar at age 83?" Edward pressed.

"No way," Michael said.

"Okay, let's move the numbers around. Suppose the average life expectancy is 86, and you had $1.5 million. Does that make a difference?"

"Nope," Michael shot right back. "We can't plan using the average life expectancy, because we don't know if our *actual* experience will fall below or above the average."

"Bingo," Edward said. "Your biggest fear is running out of money, but you have no idea how long you will live! So you spend as little as you can."

"Big barrel, small sips," Kathleen said.

Edward reached into his briefcase and removed a sheet of paper. "Traditional retirement planning forces us to recognize the difference between life *expectancy* and life *potential*."

Michael stared down at the chart as his father spoke.

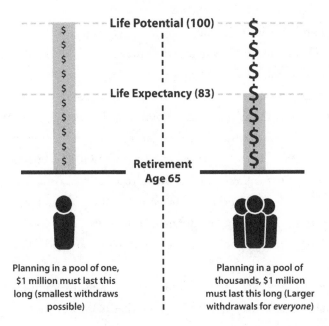

Figure 12.1

"Life *expectancy* is the age an average person will *probably* live to; about half the population will live longer," Edward said. "Life *potential* is the age an average person *could* live to. The average life expectancy might be 83, but *your* personal life potential might be 100. Since no one knows how long they are going to live, they are forced to plan to their life potential, which means they must withdraw smaller amounts of money under the *possibility* they might live to 100 or older.

Life *expectancy* is the age an average person will *probably* live to; about half the population will live longer. Life *potential* is the age an average person *could* live to.

"The rub is that retirees may or may *not* need this money," Edward added. "There is just no way to know, so they have to take small withdrawals to ensure it will last."

Edward tapped the chart. "But if a person joins a retirement pool of thousands of people, actuaries can figure out the average life expectancy of the *pool*. When they do that, they can pay out an income stream that is based on life expectancy rather than life potential. But because you are now in a pool with thousands of others, you can rest assured that if you are one of the lucky ones to live to your full life potential, that income will keep coming. Pensions are different from retirement planning because they're done in a large pool of people rather than as individuals. Efficiency can be gotten from the *pool*."

"I get it," Michael nodded. "Some people will live to 102 years old, but some will pass away at age 72. Those that pass away sooner subsidize the people who live longer."

Some people will live to 102 years old, but some will pass away at age 72. Those that pass away sooner subsidize the people who live longer.

"Exactly," Edward said. "There is a morbid term for this known as mortality credits. Those who live the longest get the 'credit' for those with shorter mortalities. I know it's a bit gloomy to think about, but in truth, under this system, *everyone* wins.

"The person who lives longer, of course, will enjoy more income," Edward went on. "But the person who lives a shorter life *also* wins because they at least had a *larger* income for the time they were alive.

"The best part about it is that when a person joins an actuarial science pool, the entity managing the pool—such as the employer or the municipality—is suddenly able to offer a guaranteed retirement income stream. By joining the pool, the longevity and volatility risks get spread among many people, so the risks are minimized. That's why actuarial science is behind all guaranteed payout streams, from Social Security to private pensions."

> **By joining the pool, the longevity and volatility risks get spread among many people, so the risks are minimized.**

"Well," Michael said. "I can see why Jill's father's girlfriend, Doris, has such a carefree retirement. She worked in the school district for 25 years, then received her pension. Guaranteed income for life." Michael shook his head. "It doesn't get any better than that."

"Actually, son, it does."

Michael regarded his father. "What do you mean?"

"Would you believe I spent a good deal of my career working with people like Doris? Working with people who had pensions?"

"Really? What did you do? I mean they don't really need any retirement planning. They have their pension."

"Would you believe I helped them make their pensions even *better*?"

Michael's Notebook:

- Actuarial science determines the average life expectancy of a pool of people.
- This dates back to the Romans, who formed groups to cover burial costs.
- Fun fact: Edmond Halley (of Halley's Comet) was one of the founding fathers of actuarial science. He set up an insurance system to determine how much money needed to be collected in premiums.
- Life expectancy = average age a person will probably live to; about half the population will live longer.
- Life potential = average age a person *could* live to.
- Traditional retirement planning in a pool of one means everyone must assume they will live to their life potential and take small withdrawals to make money last.
- Planning in a pool of many people means actuaries can create a payout to life expectancy but ensure those who live longer still get paid.
  - ◊ Some will live to 75; some will live to 105. Those who live longer are subsidized by those who die sooner (mortality credits).
- Pensions have two components:
  - ◊ Investment side
  - ◊ Guaranteed income stream (uses actuarial science)
- How do you make a pension *better*???

CHAPTER 13

PENSIONS, TAKE TWO

"How can you make a pension *better*?" Michael furrowed his brow. "Isn't your pension mostly determined for you? When you retire, you get a set amount for the rest of your life?"

"I'll admit it may seem that pensions are straightforward. Your reward for your life's work is a lifetime of income. Pensioners certainly don't face the complexity that many of today's retirees deal with. In the golden age of pensions, retirees had *two* sources of guaranteed income—their pension[1] and Social Security. These combined guaranteed *lifetime* income streams offered tremendous peace of mind for retirees. They did not have the Desert Island Problem. It didn't matter how the market performed year to year, and it did not matter how long they lived. The pension and Social Security covered that.

"What's more, retirees with pensions don't face the endless choices that nonpensioners face today. In today's retirement planning world, there are thousands of investment products and thousands of insurance products, and piecing them together is dizzying."

"Tell me about it," Michael sighed.

"But even though pensioners don't have to deal with thousands of choices, they still have to make a crucial decision on the kind of payout they elect."

Michael cocked his head. "Payout? Don't they all pay out the same? You get a check until you die?"

"Nothing could be further from the truth, son. Many people think there is only one kind of payout to a pension; the kind where you retire with a set income for life. This is known as a life-only pension. If you live for 40 years after you retire, then you'll receive 40 years' worth of income. But if you live only four *days* after you retire, then you'll receive just four days' worth of income. This is how pensions can pay out such high guaranteed incomes."

"Sure," Michael nodded. "People who die sooner subsidize the people who die later."

"Correct," Edward said. "Pensions pay the highest guaranteed payouts. But there are still many *types* of payouts within the pension to choose from. When a pensioner elects to receive a check for the rest of their life, they have chosen a payout option known as the *life-only payout option.* This option covers you for the rest of *your* life, whether that's four days or 40 years. Its primary benefit is that it offers the *highest* guaranteed payout in the pension world. But, as you can guess, this payout option has one glaring flaw."

"When you die, the payouts stop, and your spouse loses the income."

"Right. Couples quickly realized that having 100 percent of your retirement income based on the pensioner's staying alive was a risky strategy. In my experience, people who chose this option did so because they badly needed the extra income, and they *had* to take the risk. Other times the pensioner's spouse was seriously ill, and it was unlikely the pensioner would pass away first." Edward sighed. "And sadly, sometimes, the pensioner just did not pay enough attention to their retirement plans. They assumed the surviving spouse would just sell the house or reduce their lifestyle, or even move in with the kids."

"Seriously?" Michael said.

"Many people who have pensions think the pension will take care of everything. While no financial product can do everything, a pension can do a lot, if the pensioner chooses the right option."

"So there are other options?"

"Yes. The life-only payout option wasn't the only type of payout option. As you can imagine, there needed to be a payout option that protected the spouse. Another type of payout was the *joint-survivor payout option*. With this option, the income lasts as long as either spouse lives."

"Now that sounds like the better option," Michael said. "At least for married people."

"Well, remember, if a pension fund has to pay out an income until the *second* person dies, then that typically means the pension will have to make payments for a longer period of time. A joint life expectancy is longer than a single life expectancy. To compensate for this, the income to the pension owner is reduced. So the income is lower, but the surviving spouse is protected.

"The joint-survivor payout option often offered several choices for pensioners," Edward went on. "A joint-survivor 100 percent is a payout option that pays out the same income until the *last* spouse dies. If the pension was, say $3,000 a month, the pensioner would receive that amount. But upon their death, their spouse would continue receiving that $3,000 a month, until the surviving spouse died.

"Another joint-survivorship option pays out a higher initial income and then is reduced at the pensioner's death. For example, under a joint-survivorship *50 percent* payout option, the pensioner might receive $4,000 a month. But upon their death, the spouse would receive $2,000 a month. Even though the surviving spouse would receive *less* income after the pensioner's death, the pensioner would receive *more* income while they were alive."

Edward pulled out a sheet and put it on the table. Michael saw it was a simple chart comparing pension payout options.

Common Pension Payout Options

Life Only
$5,000/month pensioner
$0/month after
pensioner's death

Joint Survivorship
$3,000/month pensioner
$3,000/ month after
pensioner's death

Joint Survivorship 50%
$4,000/month pensioner
$2,000/ month after
pensioner's death

Figure 13.1

"The question," Edward said, grinning, "is which one is the best option?"

Michael smiled at another of his father's teaching moments. He had to figure it out himself.

"Well," he began, "obviously the life-only option is ideal for an unmarried person."

"Agreed."

"But it does get a bit more complicated for married folks. I mean you *can't* choose the life-only option. That would mean your entire retirement plan is based on the pensioner staying alive."

"Also agreed," Edward said.

"So it seems a married person would *have* to choose one of the joint-survivor options." Michael looked up from the sheet and shrugged. "The income from the pension has to be protected. Married people just have no other option."

Edward smiled. "Would you believe I spent a good deal of my career showing married people they have many options?"

"Arguing *for* the life-only option for married people?"

"It does offer the highest guaranteed payout, son."

"Yeah, but what about the spouse?"

"A large part of my career was spent answering that very question. I worked with firefighters, police officers, upper-level executives, and even teachers, anyone who had a pension to look forward to. For most of these folks, their pension was the most important part of their retirement plan. The choice they made locked in the amount of their retirement income for life. It was critical they knew how all the options worked and how they could *maximize* their pension. I helped them choose the *highest* guaranteed payout on their pension *and* ensured their spouse was protected with the income he or she would need for life. I did this using a strategy called Pension Maximization or Pension Max for short. Since fewer people have pensions these days, the strategy is not as well-known as it once was. In the past it was a common practice to help people maximize their pension income using the strategy."

"How did you do that?" Michael asked.

"The first step was to walk the pensioner and their spouse through the four possible life scenarios." Edward slid another sheet across the table to Michael.

FOUR POSSIBILITIES:

Pensioner dies first/early

Spouse dies first/early

Both die early

Both live a long time

"When it comes to married couples in their retirement years, there are only four possibilities to consider. One, the pensioner dies first. Two, the spouse dies first. Three, they both die early. And four, they both live a long time.

"I would guide my clients and their spouses through the four possibilities using the three most common pension payout options. I would always begin with the option that offered the highest potential payout—the life-only option."

Edward slid another chart in front of Michael. "As you can see, this option pays a generous lifetime income, as long as the pensioner remains alive. But on its own, it is too risky a strategy for the pensioner's spouse. And if the pensioner and their spouse pass away at or near the same time, there is nothing left for their heirs."[2]

Life-Only Payout
$60,000/year for pensioner, $0 for spouse

	Retirement Age	Yearly Income	# of Years of Income	Total Income	Income Loss / Gain	Legacy	Comments
Outcome 1 Both live to 90.	65	$60,000	25	$1,500,000	$0	NONE	This is the best option. Both parties live a long retirement and enjoy highest possible payout.
Outcome 2 Pensioner lives to 90. Spouse dies at 70.	65	$60,000	25	$1,500,000	$0	NONE	Highest payout when pensioner lives a long time.
Outcome 3 Spouse lives to 90. Pensioner dies at 70.	65	$60,000	5	$300,000	($1,200,000)	NONE	Large income loss when pensioner dies first. Spouse is on their own.
Outcome 4 Both die at 70.	65	$60,000	5	$300,000	($1,200,000)	NONE	Heirs lose the balance of pension.

Figure 13.2

"Of course, any pensioner would love to be able to choose the life-only option because it pays out the most. But as we've established, it's just too risky if the pensioner dies early or just dies first."

"So people needed to choose one of the joint options?" Michael asked.

"That is exactly the attitude most of my clients had at first. But this is our opportunity to learn that *all* of the payout options are possible if we prepare correctly." Edward produced another chart. "The joint-survivor options do protect against the spouse outliving the pensioner. However, this protection comes at a steep cost. In exchange for this protection, both the pensioner and the spouse many times live on the lowest income offered of all the pension payout options."

Edward pointed to the column on the chart that read *income loss*. "Compare the lifetime potential income that is surrendered from the start, against what you *could've* had by choosing the life-only option. The lost income for many might be the difference between sending holiday cards to grandchildren versus actually visiting them. Or the difference between watching the travel channel instead of doing the traveling! Over the retiree's lifetime, we are talking about hundreds of thousands of dollars lost, all in the name of protecting the spouse. And in all scenarios, the children do not get anything. In the event of an early death, the heirs cannot collect the remaining pension income."

Joint Survivorship Payout (100%)
$36,000/year for pensioner, $36,000/year for spouse

	Retirement Age	Yearly Income	# of Years of Income	Total Income	Income Loss	Legacy	Comments
Life Only	65	$60,000	25	$1,500,000	$0	NONE	This is the benchmark of comparison.
Outcome 1 Both live to 90.	65	$36,000	25	$900,000	($600,000)	NONE	If both live a long time, $600,000 in income is lost when compared to the life-only option.
Outcome 2 Pensioner lives to 90. Spouse dies at 70.	65	$36,000	25	$900,000	($600,000)	NONE	If pensioner lives a long time, $600,000 in income is lost when compared to the life-only option.
Outcome 3 Spouse lives to 90. Pensioner dies at 70.	65	$36,000	25	$900,000	$600,000	NONE	This payout option protects against the pensioner dying first. $600,000 in income is preserved when compared to the life-only option.
Outcome 4 Both die at 70.	65	$36,000	5	$180,000	($120,000)	NONE	If both die young, $120,000 in income is lost when compared to the life-only option.

Figure 13.3

"That brings us to the 50 percent survivor option. There are a few scenarios where this option makes sense. First, perhaps a couple assumes they will do most of their spending at the beginning of their retirement and that the surviving spouse will not spend as much later. Second, it might be a good choice where the pensioner is in good health and the surviving spouse has significant health issues. In that case, the couple believes the pensioner will outlive the spouse. Or perhaps the couple knows they will have a windfall like an inheritance that will cover the surviving spouse later in life. But as you can see, even if this payout option is made on purpose, there is still a risk the pensioner can die first, leaving the surviving spouse a reduced income. While the 50 percent joint-survivorship payout option provides more income for as long as the pensioner lives, it *still* does not pay out as much as the single-life option."

Joint Survivorship Payout (50%)
$48,000/year for pensioner, $24,000/year for spouse

	Retirement Age	Yearly Income	# of Years of Income	Total Income	Income Loss / Gain	Legacy	Comments
Life Only	65	$60,000	25	$1,500,000	$0	NONE	This is the benchmark of comparison.
Outcome 1 Both live to 90.	65	$48,000	25	$1,200,000	**($300,000)**	NONE	If both live a long time, $300,000 in income is lost when compared to the life-only option.
Outcome 2 Pensioner lives to 90. Spouse dies at 70.	65	$48,000	25	$1,200,000	**($300,000)**	NONE	If pensioner lives a long time, $300,000 in income is lost when compared to the life-only option.
Outcome 3 Spouse lives to 90. Pensioner dies at 70.	65	$48,000 for 5 years $24,000 for 20 years	25	$720,000	$420,000	NONE	This payout option also protects against the pensioner dying first. $420,000 in income is preserved when compared to the life-only option.
Outcome 4 Both die at 70.	65	$48,000	5	$240,000	**($120,000)**	NONE	If both die young, $120,000 in income is lost when compared to the life-only option.

Figure 13.4

Michael shuffled the three charts in his hands, taking time to study each one. "Well, if we had a crystal ball, we could see which option would be best. If we knew the pensioner outlives the spouse, we would choose the single-life option every time. But I do not know how in good conscience you could choose this option without that knowledge. I guess you just have to settle for the lower payments."

He set the charts down and folded his arms on the table.

Edward had a smile that told Michael something important was to come.

Edward said, "In a noble effort to protect their spouses, pensioners surrendered large amounts of potential lifetime income. And regardless of which payout option they chose, or which life outcome befell them, in *all* scenarios their kids never benefited from the pension."

"So how did Pension Maximization help?"

"Advisors figured out that a pension could be *maximized* by pairing a life-only payout option with a life insurance policy, and Pension Maximization was born. Before their retirement, a pensioner would purchase a permanent life insurance policy. The policy would have a death benefit calculated to be large enough to replace the income of the pensioner when the pensioner dies. And the spouse would be whole."[3]

Advisors figured out that a pension could be *maximized* by pairing a life-only payout option with a life insurance policy, and Pension Maximization was born.

Edward pointed to a chart. "Look at the joint-survivor 100 percent payout option. Financially speaking, it doesn't matter who passes away first. There will always be $36,000 worth of annual income. But the *cost* of that protection is $24,000 a year, when you compare that to the life-only option, which would have paid out $60,000 a year. This cost—the difference between the higher income of a life-only option and the lower income of a survivorship option—is sometimes referred to as a *life premium*. Essentially, when someone elects a survivorship option, they are buying a life insurance policy on the pensioner. It's basically forced insurance. The joint-survivorship options have built in this strategy, just not to the benefit of the pensioner."

Joint Survivorship 100%
$36,000/year for Pensioner, $36,000 for Spouse

	Retirement Age	Yearly Income	# of Years of Income	Total Income	Income Loss	Legacy	Comments
Life Only	65	$60,000	25	$1,500,000	$0	NONE	This is the benchmark of comparison.
Outcome 1 Both live to 90.	65	$36,000	25	$900,000	($600,000)	NONE	This is the best outcome. Both parties live a long retirement, however least amount of income for life.
Outcome 2 Pensioner lives to 90. Spouse dies at 70.	65	$36,000	25	$900,000	($600,000)	NONE	Worst outcome for pensioner. Least amount of income for life.
Outcome 3 Spouse lives to 90. Pensioner dies at 70.	65	$36,000	25	$900,000	($600,000)	NONE	This is the option we guarded against. This is the reason the income is so low.
Outcome 4 Both die at 70.	65	$36,000	5	$180,000	($1,320,000)	NONE	Least income for life. Heirs lose the balance of pension.

Figure 13.5

"So Pension Max is a process that looks at pairing the life-only option with a life insurance policy?" Michael asked.

"Exactly. Remember, when you choose a survivorship option, you are *automatically* paying a life insurance premium to protect your spouse. You're just 'paying' it in the form of agreeing to accept a lower income. If a pensioner could instead choose a life-only option accompanied by a life insurance policy that would provide enough income to the surviving spouse, then often the pension could be maximized. Often, the higher income from the life-only option more than covers the life insurance premiums."[4]

Michael nodded. "I see how that works. And I guess that the life insurance policy provided more flexibility."

"Exactly. Let's go through the four outcomes of the pension again and see how it is different with the life insurance policy." Edward produced another sheet and laid it in front of Michael.

Four possibilities:

1. **Pensioner dies first/early.** In this case, the carefully calculated death benefit will provide a lump sum or stream of payments to the surviving spouse to keep them at the same standard of living they would have had with the pension. One additional benefit is if the surviving spouse does not need the full income of the pension, there is the potential to leave a legacy to children, schools, or charities. That's a benefit the pension could never provide.

2. **Spouse dies first/early.** In this case, the pensioner would continue to earn the full and highest payout option. The pensioner has a choice of what to do with the life insurance policy. They can use the cash value in the policy to supplement their income. They could keep it to provide a legacy to loved ones or philanthropic interests. They can simply cancel the policy. In either case, the full amount of the pension will continue.

3. **Both die early.** This is the most tragic of the options. In this case, the life insurance policy will provide a legacy for the kids. In a sense, it is a way to make sure the full payout of the pension is made to *someone*. The pensioner who worked a lifetime and forfeited this income because of an early death can be glad the reward was paid to someone of their choosing.

4. **Both live a long time.** This is the best option. We get what we hoped for—a long retirement with our loved one. The couple will have enjoyed more income than the joint options offered. Some advanced benefits of a life insurance policy allow the couple to use some of the cash value to supplement their income. It is also possible to scale back the policy over time as they grow older, since they would not need as much death benefit. This could free up more dollars in retirement. Finally, the couple will still leave a legacy to their children or the charity of their choice. It is a very elegant way to have secured the most income for themselves and leave something to future generations.

Michael studied the sheet as his father said, "The key to these options is that the couple needs to ensure the correct amount of death benefit is purchased and the policy is kept in force. The life insurance policy has to stay in effect for this to work. Often paying those premiums is easy, as the additional income from the life-only payout option covers the life insurance premiums. Of course every situation is different, depending on the size of the pension, the age of the pensioner upon retirement, and other factors. But it's worth *anyone* with a pension going through the Pension Max exercise. It doesn't work every time, but it works enough to make it worth looking into."

Edward watched his son as he processed the strategy.

"Okay." Michael put down the sheet. "I understand that Pension Maximization is simply a strategy that aligns a permanent life insurance policy with a traditional pension. It allows the pensioner to elect the highest pension payout option—the life-only option—and to protect their spouse with life insurance. Rather than be subjected to the inflexible terms of one of the joint-survivor options, the pensioner has flexibility in retirement. It also provides an opportunity for the pensioner and their spouse to provide a legacy to their kids."

"I would say that is an excellent summary, son."

"I can see how Pension Maximization can help someone with a pension. But I don't have a pension, so how does it help me?"

"You're like most people these days, son. Traditional pensions have all but disappeared. But there is a way for an individual, *any* individual, to incorporate the principles of Pension Maximization into your retirement. I call it a Pension Max 2.0."

Michael smiled. "Pension Max 2.0?"

"Yep. Think about traditional pensions. They're great for generating guaranteed income, but they are pretty inflexible. As the name implies, Pension Max 2.0 is the new and improved way of creating a personal pension. Anyone can use the principles of the old Pension Max Strategy and create a private version. But the new model allows the retiree many new choices and, most important, it allows for control. It can be customized to your specific needs."

Michael leaned in. "Dad, you're killing me. How do I get my own pension?"

"There's only one place in the world you can do it."

Michael's Notebook:

- Pensions have different payout options:
  ◊ Life-only: When pensioner dies, income stream stops. (Largest payout.)
  ◊ 100 percent joint-survivor: Lower income but income continues until second spouse dies.
  ◊ 50 percent joint-survivor: Pensioner receives higher income than 100 percent joint-survivor option but lower income than life only. When pensioner dies, spouse receives 50 percent of pensioner's income.
- All pension options:
  ◊ No reimbursement for early death.
- When considering pension payout option, four possibilities:
  ◊ Pensioner dies first/early.
  ◊ Spouse dies first/early.
  ◊ Both die early.
  ◊ Both live a long time.
- Pension Maximization:
  ◊ Choose life-only payout option but protect spouse with a life insurance policy.
  ◊ Highest payout option.
  ◊ Income replenished when pensioner dies.
  ◊ If both live a long time, legacy for kids.

CHAPTER 14

THE SPIA

Michael thought about where an individual might be able to get their own pension. Impatient for his father's answer, he took a guess as to how an individual could benefit using actuarial science. "An insurance company?"

"Yes. That's what insurance companies do," Edward said. "Think of it as your own private pension. Back in the days of formal pensions, you were *automatically* thrown into a pool. That's what Doris has. But today we have to *join* one. Unless you are lucky enough to have a pension through work, there is only one place where an *individual* can partake of the benefits of actuarial science. And that is through an insurance company.

"Insurance is the only industry that uses actuarial science to pool investors together. By forming the pool, the insurance company can offer a distribution rate much higher than what an individual could withdraw from their retirement account alone. The distribution rate can sometimes be more than *double* what a balance-sheet-*only* withdrawal can offer.

Insurance is the only industry that uses actuarial science to pool investors together.

"And," Edward added, "it's guaranteed."[1]

He handed his son another sheet of paper. It was a simple chart comparing two retirement strategies. Option 1 was a retirement option offered by insurance companies. Option 2 was the traditional systematic withdrawal strategy.[2]

Actuarial science vs systematic withdrawal

	Withdrawal Rate	Actuarial Science?	Income Guaranteed?
Option 1 (Actuarial Science)	7%[3]	Yes	Yes
Option 2 (Systematic Withdrawal Strategy)	3%	No	No

Edward pointed at the chart. "As you can see, Option 1 offers a withdrawal rate roughly double that of the systematic withdrawal strategy. And the income is guaranteed.[4] The simple reason that payout is so high is because Option 1 takes advantage of actuarial science by inclusion in a pool of thousands. Option 2 involves planning in a pool of one."

"This is really exciting," Michael said. "I can see how my retirement income stream skyrockets using actuarial science. So how do I get this option?"

"Actually, you *already* have one form of it. Your whole-life insurance policy. Life insurance is one financial product that utilizes the power of actuarial science."

Michael smiled at his father. "That policy just keeps popping up, doesn't it?"

"Stick around. You haven't seen the last of it." He winked. "Now let's look at another financial product that uses actuarial science.

"In this example," Edward pointed to the sheet, "the product that pays out a guaranteed 7 percent for life is a specific type of annuity.

"When you buy an annuity, the insurance company guarantees you an income for a certain period of time. The annuity is secured by a contract with an insurance company. Depending on the annuity, that period of time might be five years, 10 years, or even a lifetime.

"There are hundreds of different annuities available today, but the one we are talking about in this example is known as a *life-only Single-Premium Immediate Annuity* or SPIA."

"Spee-uh?" Michael repeated.

"That's right. The life-only SPIA works like this: You give the insurance company a lump sum of money. That lump sum could be any amount you want—$100,000, $500,000, a million, or more. In exchange for that lump sum, the company agrees to pay you a fixed percentage of that money every year, for the rest of your life. The life-only SPIA uses actuarial science in its purest form. That's why it offers the highest *guaranteed* payout rate.

> **The life-only SPIA uses actuarial science in its purest form. That's why it offers the highest *guaranteed* payout rate.**

"If you bought a $100,000 annuity with a 7 percent payout, you would receive $7,000 a year for the rest of your life. If you bought a $1 million annuity with a 7 percent payout, you would receive $70,000 a year for the rest of your life, regardless of how long you live."

"That's Doris's favorite line," Michael said. "'*If I live to be 110 years old, that's my pension's problem, not mine.*'"

"She's right," Edward said. "With a life-only SPIA, the insurance company is taking all the risk for volatility and longevity, *and* they are offering a distribution rate that's potentially more than *twice* what the safe withdrawal rate is."

"How can they do that?"

"We have to remember how this strategy works," Edward said. "At retirement, you are going to have to exchange a lump sum of money for a *guaranteed* income stream for as long as you live."

Michael sat up. "Wait a minute. So, if I live to be 100 years old, that's great. But if I bought a life-only SPIA and then passed away in six months, I would lose everything? My kids would get *nothing*?"

"Son," Edward said calmly, "I would *never* recommend a strategy that disinherits your family."

"I hope not," Kathleen said.

"So, what's the catch?"

"No catch." Edward gave him a wry smile. "Remember that whole-life insurance policy you're so keen to get rid of?"

"Yeah."

"Well, that whole-life insurance policy can also make the SPIA even *better* than a traditional pension with Pension Max."

Michael's Notebook:

- Insurance companies can let individuals make use of actuarial science. (In the past, a pension put people into pools.)

- An annuity is a contract with an insurance company. There are many different types, but one that uses actuarial science is the life-only single-premium immediate annuity or life-only SPIA.

- The life-only SPIA trades a lump sum of money for a guaranteed lifetime income stream.

  ◊ Example: Buy a $1 million life-only SPIA with a 7 percent payout rate, get $70,000 a year, *guaranteed* for as long as you live.

- One drawback to SPIA:

  ◊ Whatever money you trade to the insurance company you surrender upon your death.

- But life insurance can protect that???

CHAPTER 15

PENSION MAX 2.0

The group finished lunch and repositioned their workstations to finish the final side of the barn. Michael climbed back onto his ladder. "So life insurance can help the life-only SPIA become *better* than a traditional pension?"

"Absolutely. Remember the goal of Pension Maximization is to get the highest payout rate possible," Edward said. "Remember that traditional pensions offer different income options. But the highest guaranteed payout is found in the life-only option.

"That option allows the pensioner to receive their *full* pension income, for life. This option is terrific for generating lifelong income, but the drawback is that to maximize the income, you must agree that the income will stop when you die. This has to happen. That's what actuarial science is all about. Those who die sooner support those who live longer. But it's definitely a drawback. That's why very few married pensioners ever choose the life-only option; they do not want to leave their spouse without the income. So, they choose an option that continues for both of their lives. As a result, their lifelong payout is lower."

"But they can often maximize that pension by choosing the life-only option and supplementing it with a life insurance policy," Michael added.

"Correct. Depending on the pensioner's age and health and particular financial situation, Pension Maximization can help them choose the highest payout option—the life-only option—*and* ensure their spouse has a lifelong income. And, remember, unlike the pension survivorship options, which offer zero chance at legacy, a life-only pension with life insurance may just leave a nice nest egg to the kids.

"The life-only SPIA is like a personal pension," Edward went on. "It offers the *highest* guaranteed retirement income stream anywhere in the financial or insurance world. So it's a great strategy for people looking for high levels of guaranteed income. Of course, that guarantee is based on the financial strength of the insurance company.

The life-only SPIA is like a personal pension.

"But the major drawback to the life-only SPIA is the same as it is for a life-only pension. To have the highest guaranteed payout, you have to agree that the moment you pass away, the insurance company gets to keep the money you exchanged to them. If you die after 40 years, you certainly got your money's worth. But you could die after just four months, so we need to protect against this one major downside. And the good news is that you already have the tool to protect against that downside."

"My whole-life insurance?" Michael smiled.

"Yes," Edward nodded. "If we can match up a life insurance death benefit with an equal amount of life-only SPIA, we negate the major downside of the life-only SPIA. The retiree would live off the income of the SPIA, then when they passed away, every dollar they traded to the insurance company for the SPIA would be replaced by the death benefit from the life insurance policy."

"So if I bought a life insurance policy today, with, say, a $500,000 death benefit, upon retirement I would buy a $500,000 life-only SPIA?" Michael asked.

"That's right," Edward said. "By buying the SPIA, you would be purchasing the highest guaranteed retirement income stream you could find anywhere. And you would be assured that the moment you passed away, the dollars you exchanged would be replenished by the life insurance policy."

"So we buy the life insurance *now* and the SPIA *later?*" Michael asked.

"Correct," Edward said. "SPIAs and life insurance are opposites. With a SPIA, a person is looking to maximize *income*. With a life insurance policy, a person is looking to minimize *premiums*. The *older* a person is when they buy a SPIA, the better the payout rate. The *younger* a person is when they buy a life insurance policy, the lower the premium. Since everyone is one day closer to not being insurable, it makes sense to buy the life insurance as soon as possible."

> SPIAs and life insurance are opposites.
> With a SPIA, a person is looking to maximize
> *income*. With a life insurance policy, a person
> is looking to minimize *premiums*.

Michael looked at his father. He saw now why the old man had pushed so hard for him and Jill to purchase whole-life policies when they first got married. He was beginning to see the versatile power of the policy. "So that life insurance policy can help me to create my very own Pension Max 2.0."

"Even better," his father said. "Don't forget, traditional pensions are subject to labor negotiations, corporate greed, and political ambition. And, more than we want to admit, these pensions have failed. That does not happen with a SPIA. And with a SPIA, a person can create their own parameters. Essentially, we are buying units of guaranteed income, so the question is, how many units do you want to buy?"

"When I heard about the SPIA," Kathleen grinned, "I said, 'I'll take as much as I can get!'"

"I raised a smart one." Edward smiled. "The thing about the SPIA combined with life insurance is technically it's *not* a pension. With a traditional pension, the pensioner gets whatever has been built up. They get what they get. But with Pension Max 2.0, we can design how much income we need or want. We can buy enough income to cover our entire lifestyle. Or we can buy just enough to cover our basic needs. We even have the flexibility of deciding when it will start.

"It's also elegant in its legacy design," Edward went on. "By combining the SPIA with life insurance, we know our money will be replenished if we pass away early. But if we live a long time, we get the benefit of the SPIA income *and* our kids will get the benefit of the life insurance. Sadly, most retirees have to choose between having an enjoyable retirement or leaving a legacy. With Pension Max 2.0, we get both. We never disinherit our spouse or our kids *and* we have the guaranteed income we want. That's the elegance of this strategy."

Kathleen watched as her brother nodded his head, processing the information. Then she noticed Michael frown. He set down his paintbrush, crossed his arms, and furrowed his brow.

Kathleen laughed to herself. She knew what was coming; her husband had arrived at this place not too long ago.

"I understand how the life-only SPIA can pay out a better rate and how a permanent life insurance policy covers the SPIA," Michael said. "But there are three problems." He held up his fingers as he spoke. "Number one, there have to be fees associated with a product like a SPIA. Number two, when you buy a SPIA, you lose all your liquidity. Once you trade that money to the insurance company, it's gone! And number three, the SPIA doesn't adjust for inflation, does it?"

"Great questions." Edward surveyed the barn. "I'd say we have another hour or so of painting, and then we're done. After that, I'll address your concerns." He looked at his son and smiled. "I think the answers might surprise you."

Michael's Notebook:

- Whole-life insurance mitigates the one downside of a life-only SPIA. Together, purchasing these two policies becomes Pension Max 2.0.

- Pension Max 2.0 strategy:
   ◊ Purchase a whole-life insurance policy in your 20s, 30s, 40s, or 50s. This policy has a death benefit.
   ◊ Then upon retirement, purchase a life-only SPIA equal to the amount of the life insurance death benefit.

Example:

- At age 45, purchase a whole-life policy with a $500,000 death benefit.

- At age 67, retire and purchase a $500,000 SPIA paying 7 percent for life guaranteed ($35,000/ year).[1]

- Upon death, the $500,000 life insurance policy replaces the money surrendered to the insurance company.

- What about:
   ◊ Fees?
   ◊ Liquidity?
   ◊ Inflation?

CHAPTER 16

UPSIDE DOWNSIDES

They spent another hour painting. By late afternoon they had finished. They circled the structure, inspecting their handiwork. When Edward was satisfied, he turned to his children.

"Well, look at that. Two full days and she's looking brand new. Thank you both for all your help. This would have taken me forever on my own."

"Happy to help," Kathleen said.

"And I appreciate you two helping me change the way I view my retirement," Michael said. "Easily a fair trade."

"Well, I think we've earned a cocktail hour," Edward said.

* * *

Ten minutes later, with drinks in hand, they gathered around the picnic table for one final discussion.

"We were talking about the life-only SPIA," Edward said. "Son, you pointed out the three common misconceptions."

Michael pulled out his notebook. "Yeah, I wrote them down. The first problem is there is no liquidity. The second problem is that the life-only

SPIA does not keep up with inflation. And the third problem is that a product as enticing as that has to have some pretty hefty fees."

Edward nodded. "The first thing we need to remember," he said, "is that there are hundreds of different types of annuities. Some have a built-in provision to keep up with inflation. Others have high fees. But what we are talking about here is the life-only SPIA. Okay?"

"Fair enough," Michael said.

"Let's look at each issue separately, starting with liquidity. There is a difference between *liquidity* and *accessibility*. *Liquidity* means an investment can easily be converted into cash. *Accessibility* means a person can actually *use* that cash. It's possible to have an investment that has liquidity but *not* accessibility.

> *Liquidity* **means an investment can easily be converted into cash.** *Accessibility* **means a person can actually** *use* **that cash.**

"When a person buys a life-only SPIA, the money they handed over to the insurance company instantly becomes *illiquid*. They cannot access those dollars anymore. The dollars belong to the insurance company now."

"Like I said, no liquidity," Michael shrugged.

"There is no more liquidity with the dollars they traded," Edward agreed. "But with a life-only SPIA in your retirement plan, you might become more liquid *overall*."

Edward reached into his briefcase and handed Michael a sheet of paper. "Let me give you an example. Let's assume we want an annual retirement income of $100,000 per year," Edward said. "Because the systematic withdrawal strategy limits how much money we can safely withdraw each year, we're going to need quite a big nest egg to generate that income. If we assume a safe withdrawal rate of 3 percent per year, then that means in order to generate $100,000 worth of income, we need to save $3,333,000 in assets."

Michael looked down at the chart. It was an expansion of a previous chart his father had shown him. Now it added two additional columns: "Assets Needed to Create 100k of Income" and "Money NOT Required for Income."

Liquidity and accessibility (systematic withdrawal strategy)

	Withdrawal Rate	Actuarial Science?	Income Guaranteed?	Assets Needed to Create $100k of Income	Money NOT Required for Income
Systematic Withdrawal Strategy	3%	NO	NO	$3,333,000	$0

"Let me ask you," Edward pointed at the chart. "The $3.3 million in assets, is it liquid?"

"Yes," Michael said. "You can sell those assets at any time and get the cash."

"I agree. Now here's another question: Is that $3.3 million *accessible?*"

Michael looked at his sister, then at his father. "What's the difference?"

"What happens if you had to take money out of that $3.3 million portfolio for an emergency?" Edward watched his son as he stared at the chart. Then he saw the light bulb go on.

"Ahhh," Michael said. "My income goes down."

"Correct," Edward said. "The money *is* liquid, but it is not *accessible,* because you need every dime of it to generate $100,000 in income.

"Now let's turn our attention to the SPIA." Edward slid another chart across the picnic table. "We can see from this chart, that the income from the SPIA *is* guaranteed."

	Withdrawal Rate	Actuarial Science?	Income Guaranteed?	Assets Needed to Create $100k of Income	Money NOT Required for Income
SPIA-Life Only	7%	YES	YES	$1,400,000	$1,900,000

Michael nodded.

"In order to generate $100,000 in income, we need to invest $1.4 million into a SPIA. Let me ask you the same question. Is that $1.4 million liquid?"

"No," Michael said. "Once you hand it over to the insurance company, you cannot get it back."

"Correct. Now let me ask the second question. Is that $1.4 million *accessible?*"

"No. You cannot get it back."

"Correct," Edward said.

"But I still don't get it," Michael said. "Where's the liquidity?"

"When we put the strategies side by side, you'll see." Edward slid one final sheet across the table.

Liquid money and accessible money
(systematic withdrawal strategy vs. life-only SPIA)

	Withdrawal Rate	Actuarial Science?	Income Guaranteed?	Assets Needed to Create $100k of Income	Money Not Required for Income	Liquid Money	Accessible Money
Systematic Withdrawal Strategy	3%	No	No	$3,333,000	$0	$3.3 million	$0
SPIA-Life Only	7%	Yes	Yes	$1,400,000	$1,900,000	$1,900,000	$1,900,000

"With the systematic withdrawal strategy, we need *all* $3.3 million to generate an annual income of $100,000. That income is *possible*, but not *guaranteed*. Technically, the assets are *liquid;* you can sell them if you want. But what happens to your income when you do?"

"Your income will go down?" Michael guessed.

"That's right. If we have to access any of that money for *any* reason, we have, by definition, reduced our income *forever*. Therefore, the funds in my retirement are *liquid* but they're not—"

"Accessible," Michael said, suddenly getting it.

"Exactly. In a sense, these assets are 'locked.' They have to stay invested to generate your retirement income.

"Now let's look at the SPIA."

Michael focused again on the chart.

	Withdrawal Rate	Actuarial Science?	Income Guaranteed?	Assets Needed to Create $100k of Income	Money Not Required for Income	Liquid Money	Accessible Money
Systematic Withdrawal Strategy	3%	No	No	$3,333,000	$0	$3.3 million	$0
SPIA-Life Only	7%	Yes	Yes	$1,400,000	$1,900,000	$1,900,000	$1,900,000

"Because the SPIA payout rate is 7 percent, we only need $1.4 million to generate the same $100,000 in income. And that income is guaranteed. This money is not liquid, and it is not accessible.

"But since we need a lot less money to generate our income goal, we have $1.9 million that is *not* required to create that income. It can be used for anything, including more income! So that $1.9 million is both . . . "

"Liquid *and* accessible," Michael said.

"You got it. So one last question, which of these two options gives you the best *overall* liquidity and accessibility?"

"Clearly," Michael said, "the SPIA option."

"Congratulations." Kathleen clanked her cocktail glass against her brother's beer bottle. "You have just learned how an SPIA creates liquidity *and* accessibility."

Michael took a sip of his beer and nodded. He couldn't argue with the math.

"Okay, I get how the SPIA creates liquidity, but what about inflation?" Michael pointed at the second bullet point in his notebook. "With the SPIA, I'll admit, the distribution rate is higher. But it's *fixed*. If inflation explodes, wouldn't the person holding the SPIA be in trouble? A million-dollar stock portfolio, on the other hand, has a chance to keep up with inflation."

"Inflation does appear to be an issue with the SPIA," Edward said. "To get the highest payout, the initial distribution from the SPIA will be very high, but it will remain the same for life. At some point, the effects of inflation will eat into the income.[1] But the SPIA is actually a good inflation hedge.

"Imagine two couples with very different $1 million portfolios. One couple keeps their portfolio in the markets and withdraws 3 percent per year. The other couple puts their money into a SPIA that pays out 7 percent.

"The couple with the stock portfolio does have some inflation protection with their stocks," Edward explained. "Their income will grow with inflation, but their income starts at only $30,000 a year. The couple with the SPIA won't see their income grow with inflation; it is fixed by the SPIA distribution rate. But the SPIA couple *starts* with $70,000 worth of guaranteed income per year.

"If inflation is averaging 3 percent per year," he continued, "it will take the systematic withdrawal couple 30 *years* to catch up to the SPIA couple. That's 30 years of extra income that can be used to invest back in the market or to enjoy in retirement."

"When I heard that, I was like, ummmm, I'll just enjoy the extra money," Kathleen smiled.

"But that's not even the biggest inflation benefit," Edward grinned. "Remember that the SPIA required only *half* the money to generate $100,000 worth of retirement income?"

"Sure."

"Well, what could you do with the rest of the money that is not needed?"

"Invest it?" Michael offered.

"Exactly! When your income from the SPIA is no longer enough because of inflation, you could buy *another* SPIA and voila! More guaranteed income. And remember, the later in life you buy a SPIA, the higher the payout rate will be. That means it will take even *less* money to create the same income the market will produce. And then you can invest the rest and repeat the cycle."

Michael nodded. He had to agree with the logic. More income is more income, pure and simple. Then his eyes fell on the last bullet point in his notebook.

Fees.

"So what about fees?" Michael said. "You say a $1.4 million dollar SPIA generates $100,000 worth of income, but how much of that $1.4 million goes toward fees?"

"Nothing," Edward said.

"Nothing?" Michael repeated.

"I know, right?" Kathleen said.

"Dad, it can't be nothing."

"Not a dime. Remember, there are many different types of annuities and many of them do have fees. I like the SPIA because it does not have any fees."

"But how is that possible?"

Edward sipped his beer. "At its core, the SPIA is a distribution product that transfers risk. Not every dollar given to the insurance company will be paid back. That's the nature of insurance. The benefit to the retiree is that they get an income much higher than they would have if they were on their own. If they live for another 50 years, that's the insurance company's problem.

"The benefit to the insurance company is that they know they will not have to pay everyone 100 percent of the money they put in. The funds the insurance company takes in but does not need to pay out is how they stay in business. The SPIA is perhaps the purest form of actuarial science."

"So if I hand the insurance company $1.4 million," Michael said, "the *entire* $1.4 million goes toward the SPIA?"

"Correct," Edward said. "No hidden fees."

"For me, Pension Max 2.0 is ideal," Kathleen said. "I'll get lifelong guaranteed income using less money, and when I die, all the dollars I invested in the SPIA will be replenished with my life insurance policy."

Michael took a long sip of his beer and looked at his father and sister.

"I think I'm starting to see the value of my whole-life policy."

Michael's Notebook:

- There are many different types of annuities (some with fees, some with built-in inflation protection).
  - ◊ Life-only SPIA is a specific type of annuity that offers the highest guaranteed payout.
- The difference between *liquidity* and *accessibility*:
  - ◊ *Liquidity* is an investment that can easily be converted into cash.
  - ◊ *Accessibility* means we can actually *use* that cash.
  - ◊ It's possible to be liquid but *not* accessible.
- Life-only SPIA *creates* liquidity by generating *more* income *with* fewer dollars.
- SPIA is also a good inflation hedge. It creates more income immediately. That income can be used to protect against inflation.
- SPIA has no fees!!!

CHAPTER 17

THE FIFTH OPTION

The trio cleaned up the job site in silence.

Edward focused his attention on Michael, watching as his son folded the tarps and double-checked that the lid was secure on the last paint can. He smiled at the ease his son applied to the tasks. His shoulders had relaxed. He had a smile on his face. Michael's demeanor was a far cry from the man who had showed up the previous morning. *That* man was terrified his retirement wouldn't work out. *That* man was frustrated that he had sacrificed for so long for nothing. *That* man didn't see a way out of his situation.

But in two days, everything had shifted.

Edward knew the last two days were a flood of information. Not just additional information to add on to what his son already knew, but also new ideas to wash away the B.S. retirement thinking that would have plagued his son until his last day. By revealing strategies that his son never knew existed, Edward had eliminated that all too common retirement planning anxiety.

Michael took off his painting overalls and hung them on the hook. "Well, Dad, I gotta say, you've changed *everything*. Honestly, I came here yesterday about to make a desperate move to save my retirement."

Edward raised his hand. "I'll say it again. Whatever you decide to do with your whole-life insurance policies, I will respect your decision."

Michael shook his head. "Nah, I see now that those whole-life policies are the *key* to the Fifth Option. They are what will spring me from the prison of the safe withdrawal rate. They are the key to overcoming the Frustrating Four options that our advisor suggested."

"Give us your three takeaways." Kathleen hung her overalls next to the ones her brother had worn.

Michael thought for a moment. "Okay. I would say number one, a Fifth Option exists outside of the Frustrating Four. When we focus on safely increasing the withdrawal rate, everything changes. And what's great is that there is a strategy for everyone. Me, I'm more of a market guy—a Beat the Bear guy. I'm drawn to the idea that there may be a big upside. My wife, on the other hand, is probably more of a Pension Max 2.0 retiree. She'll want the guaranteed income. And for those in the middle, there's the Bucket Strategy."

When we focus on safely increasing the withdrawal rate, everything changes.

Michael put away his ladder. "Number two, I would say that more money *isn't* the solution. That's B.S. thinking. The real problem is *income*."

More money *isn't* the solution. That's B.S. thinking. The real problem is *income*.

"And number three?" Kathleen helped her brother with the tall ladder she'd been using.

"Easy. Number three would be actuarial science. When we get out of this idea of planning retirement all alone and get *into* this idea of planning as part of a group, everything changes."

> **When we get out of this idea of planning retirement all alone and get *into* this idea of planning as part of a group, everything changes.**

* * *

An hour later, Michael was in his driveway hugging his sister goodbye.

"How did it go?" Jill asked. "I want to hear all about it. We have time."

"Grab a drink and have a seat," Michael smiled.

A beer in hand, Michael took his wife through all he had learned during the past two days. Then he reminded his wife where they had started. "Since we don't have pensions, we are on our own, on a path of minimal retirement income. We were trying to plan for two things we could not plan for—longevity and volatility. With the systematic withdrawal strategy, we could counter those risks, but we would be forced to take out only very small amounts from our retirement fund every year.

"Of course, you and I didn't like that. But our advisor said there were only four options: Save more. Work longer. More risk. Or lower expectations.

"Now thanks to my dad, we know about a Fifth Option. It's a combination of investing in the markets and using insurance products to efficiently generate income."

"It's not about a big pile of money," Jill said. "It's about *income*."

"There are different strategies to achieve that," Michael added. "Personally, I like the Beat the Bear Strategy," Michael said. "Most of my money is still in the markets, which means I'll have exposure to the huge upside potential. But if there is a down year, I'll have a few years of cushion in my life insurance policy that I can dip into. I don't have to worry because my life insurance cash account is growing *separate* from the markets. It's guaranteed *and* it's tax-free."[1]

Michael looked at his wife. "How about you?"

Jill took a sip of wine and thought for a moment. "Actually, I am thinking of a bit of a hybrid strategy. I like the idea that Pension Max 2.0 provides a guaranteed income for life and that any money I trade for a life-only SPIA will be covered by the death benefit from my life insurance policy.

"But," Jill raised a finger, "I understand that with a SPIA, the *later* in life I buy it, the better the payout rate will be. So, for the first 10 years of my retirement, I think the Bucket Strategy works for me. I can create a 10-year block of guaranteed and predictable income in my Now and Soon Buckets, while a large portion of my retirement fund will be growing in the Later Bucket. Then, when I am older, I can make the jump to a Pension Max 2.0."

"That's the beauty of it, hon," agreed Michael. "As long as we keep those life insurance policies, we don't have to choose now. We don't even have to make a permanent choice in our retirement. I can employ the Beat the Bear Strategy then switch to Pension Max 2.0 when it makes sense."

"And to think, we thought the answer was *canceling* those policies."

Michael smiled. At the time they purchased those policies, he'd thought they were just life insurance to replace his income or his wife's if they passed away during their *working* years. He never considered just how valuable life insurance could be during their *retirement* years.

Michael felt a bit sorry for folks who would never learn about the Fifth Option. They would keep pounding away, working, saving, risking, and sacrificing, without ever realizing they were trying to plan against the unknowable. They would never know there was a better way.

Jill interrupted his thoughts. "I'm so glad you went to visit your father.

Now we *can* have the retirement we want. We just need to save more *efficiently* to maximize our retirement income streams."

"We now have the Fifth Option. We have left the safe withdrawal rate behind."

The doorbell rang.

Jill looked at her watch. "Wow, they're early."

Michael cocked his head. "Who's early?"

Jill looked at her husband. "Michael, it's the last Sunday of the month. We have dinner with Ron and Yewende."

Michael smacked his forehead. With all that had happened in the last two days, he had totally forgotten.

They got up and opened the door for Ron and Yewende Miller, whom they'd met when they first moved to town. Yewende was their family's dentist, and Ron's company had done their kitchen renovation.

"I know we're early," Yewende said. "I'm sorry."

"No problem." Jill gave Yewende a hug.

"My fault." Ron raised a hand. "I just wasn't going to stay another minute in that meeting."

"We just met with our financial advisor," Yewende explained. "It did not go well."

"It just seems like the advice we keep hearing is the same old B.S." Ron shook his head.

"That's *exactly* the problem, Ron," Michael said. "Traditional retirement planning is 100 percent B.S."

Ron cocked his head.

"You know," Michael smiled. "'B.S.' as in balance sheet."

Yewende lifted her brow. "What are you . . . "

Jill ushered them into the living room. "Come on in. It's going to be an interesting dinner."

LET'S END THE CIVIL WAR

W e began this book by stating that the characters in the story are not real, but their problems are. Michael and Jill Cunningham represent the tens of millions of Americans who are unnecessarily struggling with their retirement planning. They have been trying to fix their financial problems with only *half* the available tools. They have been living their entire financial lives following only one financial army—the investment army. They had been told in no uncertain terms that they were at war with the other army—the insurance army.

In generations past, the retirement system worked for one simple reason: The two camps weren't at odds. Instead, they worked *together* to create safe, predictable, and plentiful retirement income streams. Pension funds realized that investments and insurance *each* had distinct benefits and drawbacks. By taking the best of both, millions of Americans were able to enjoy a comfortable, worry-free retirement.

Sadly, over time, these two sides began to battle each other. There were books and gurus and infomercials with experts from *both* sides, each proclaiming that not only was *their* army better than the other, there was *no need* for the other army at all.

"Put 100 percent of your money into insurance!" shouted one side.

"No!" cried the other side. "Invest 100 percent of your money in the markets!" A vicious information war began, and the consumer lost.

One need only look at the dismal retirement facts that plague our nation. People are being told to save more than ever and to get by with less. They are being told to work longer and limit their expectations. They are told to make difficult sacrifices, and all for no good reason.

The sacrifices are unnecessary, because there is a solution. There has *always* been a solution. The solution is to *merge* the best aspects of investment with the best aspects of insurance. That's what *The Fifth Option* is all about.

The corporate pensions of the past may be gone forever, but individuals can drastically improve their retirement when they accept the simple concept that when it comes to retirement planning, investments work better when combined with actuarial science, and actuarial science works better when combined with an investment strategy. While there are many different products in each world, and each individual retirement plan is different, the eternal concept of taking the best of *both* will allow individuals to have the retirement they always dreamed of.

There are a vast array of suboptions among the plethora of financial and insurance products available. There are many different types of annuities, life insurance policies, and investment products that work with different strategies and buckets. And, of course, some folks will incorporate other assets like real estate or business income into their retirement plans. Many of *The Fifth Option* strategies can be combined with each other to create just the right mix for your unique circumstance.

We hope this book has broadened your knowledge and the ability to increase your retirement income streams, but we also hope the book will become the impetus for national change. Rather than continuing the senseless all-or-nothing battle between investment and insurance, we want to foster conversations in cafes and at kitchen tables, in financial planning offices, and around water coolers everywhere. We want those conversations to turn into action.

Once people realize that they are not forced to plan their retirement in a pool of one, that they do *not* have to take 100 percent of the risk and make 100 percent of the sacrifice themselves, we will, as a nation, move to a state of true, lasting abundance for all.

APPENDIX

THE STRATEGIES

The book discussed four retirement income strategies:

- Systematic Withdrawal Strategy
- Beat the Bear
- Bucket Strategy
- Pension Max 2.0

In this Appendix, we offer additional insights for each of the strategies and frequently asked questions.

SYSTEMATIC WITHDRAWAL STRATEGY

This strategy has been the gold standard ever since William Bengen helped identify how much market volatility impacts our retirement income streams. His research explained the conundrum of why a retiree who is averaging an 8 percent return cannot safely withdraw 6 percent. Bengen's findings forced us to recognize that beyond Social Security and the rare pension, most Americans have an uncertain retirement outcome. The financial planning industry has put the weight of increasing retirement income squarely on the shoulders of individuals, without teaching them how retirement income streams really work.

- **Income:** Recommended 2.7 to 4 percent withdrawals per year
- **Guarantees:** None
- **Best for:**
  - Retirees who are comfortable with volatility and market management
  - Retirees with larger asset bases
- **Not for:**
  - Retirees who dislike volatility
  - Retirees who do not want to constantly manage balances throughout retirement
- **Advantages:**
  - Retirees maintain total control of investments
  - If there are long sustained bull markets, retirees might have a chance of a larger ending legacy
  - Works well for retirees with larger asset bases and smaller income requirements
- **Disadvantages:**
  - Least predictable income
  - Least efficient income production
  - Can deplete quickly in down markets
  - Must control behavior even during the hardest of times
  - Requires constant monitoring
  - Most susceptible to aging mental capacity issues
  - May have less liquidity than you think, due to large requirement of assets pledged to generate income
  - Unknown legacy

BEAT THE BEAR

This is the first of *The Fifth Option* strategies that helps mitigate the damaging effects of volatility. By separating some retirement funds, such as cash value life insurance, we create a safe place to withdraw funds in a down market. Three to four years of income in noncorrelated assets can significantly increase your withdrawal rate without the corresponding risk.

- **Income:** With 3 to 4 years of separated income, a 6 percent withdrawal rate will have a risk level compared to a 2.5 to 4 percent withdrawal rate from a 100 percent market portfolio

- **Guarantees:** None

- **Best for:**
    - Retirees with more than five years until retirement
    - Retirees comfortable with volatility
    - Retirees with larger asset bases
    - Retirees wanting some guaranteed legacy
    - Retirees who already have permanent cash value policies

- **Not for:**
    - Retirees who dislike volatility
    - Retirees who do not want to constantly manage balances throughout retirement
    - Retirees with emotional reactions to volatility

- Retirees who are uninsurable
- Retirees within 5 years of retirement

- **Advantages:**
  - Statistically possible to increase withdrawal rate above safe withdrawal rate without increasing risk
  - Good for retirees with less aggressive asset bases
  - Works well for retirees with larger asset bases and smaller income requirements
  - If there are long sustained bull markets retirees might have a chance of a larger ending legacy

- **Disadvantages:**
  - No guaranteed income
  - Depending on the market experience and portfolio structure, may have a small asset base at start of retirement
  - Market is still primary source of income
  - Must still manage retirement assets
  - Buffered amount can be depleted if too many down markets are experienced
  - Improved potential legacy

BUCKET STRATEGY

The Bucket Strategy introduces three key concepts. 1) A preservation phase designed to eliminate the most dangerous period of retirement—the few years before and after retirement; 2) allocating dollars to jobs and time lines for those jobs allows retirees to choose best product for the job of those dollars; 3) having rolling 3-, 5-, and 10-year periods where income is satisfied independent of market volatility (no need to sell market gains for income).

- **Income:** Recommended 2.5 to 4 percent withdrawals per year

- **Guarantees:** Can be for periods of 3, 5, 10 years or a lifetime

- **Best for:**
  - Retirees within five years of retirement or who have retired
  - Retirees looking to retire early
  - Retirees who have time before other guaranteed income streams turn on
  - Retirees with serious health conditions

- **Not for:**
  - Older retirees who will qualify for a high-payout SPIA

- **Advantages:**
  - Reduces overall effects of volatility
  - Allows for more aggressive portfolio structure in later buckets
  - Can make use of any type of guaranteed income options
  - Works well for retirees with larger asset bases and smaller income requirements
  - Works well as a bridge to purchasing a SPIA at a later date

- **Disadvantages:**
  - Does not, on its own, increase the withdrawal rate; only makes withdrawals safer during the 3, 5-, or 10-year "bridge" period
  - Still requires monitoring of investments
  - No guaranteed legacy unless life insurance is incorporated

PENSION MAX 2.0

Pension Max 2.0 resembles a true pension that incorporates the most actuarial science. The SPIA acts as the income-for-life vehicle, and the life insurance acts as the backstop in case of early death to provide the pledged assets back to the surviving spouse or children.

- **Income:** Highest guaranteed income for life
- **Guarantees:** Yes

- **Best for:**
  - Retirees looking for guaranteed income throughout retirement
  - Most efficient manner to generate income over long periods of time
  - Retirees with more than 5 years until retirement
  - Retirees not interested in managing large sums of money into retirement
  - Retirees interested in providing a legacy
  - Provides true liquidity

- **Not for:**
  - Retirees who want control of their money at all times
  - Young retirees

- **Advantages:**
  - Guaranteed income for life
  - Eliminates impact of volatility to income
  - Allows for more aggressive portfolio structure
  - Can make use of any type of guaranteed-income options
  - Lowest monitoring commitment
  - Takes advantage of mortality credits

- **Disadvantages:**
  - Payout rates tied to age (usually must be older than 70 for payouts to be attractive)
  - Can be challenging for people with modest balance sheets
  - Less attractive for those who do not have/cannot get life insurance
  - Less attractive for those with serious health issues

A WORD ON MONTE CARLO SIMULATIONS

As we mentioned before, you will encounter financial experts who will refute the recommended safe withdrawal rate. They will scoff at numbers like 2.5 percent and 3 percent and instead claim a 4, 5, or even 6 percent withdrawal is possible. Not only that, they will be able to back up their data with a chart. They will show you that under *their* simulation, a 5 or even 6 percent withdrawal rate is a safe number to take out over a 30-year period.

We want to remind readers that Monte Carlo is merely a data-analysis program. You get out what you put in. The program can be run using 10-year periods of market data, 100-year periods of market data, or anything in between. What's more, highs and lows can be cut out to skew the numbers in a certain direction. Tweak a little here and a little there, and presto! you can safely increase your withdrawal rate.

It might work. In many of the Monte Carlo simulations it does work. But, as the old adage goes, "plan for the worst, not the best." The only way to know for certain if the withdrawal rate you choose works is with hindsight. Most of us will act like the desperate castaway on the desert island, staring at our big bucket of water, but only taking small sips. The consequences of being wrong are just too great.

The good news is that while today's retirees have a greater exposure to volatility and longevity risks, they also have the Fifth Option to combat them!

WHAT THE CHARTS DON'T SHOW

Another factor to consider—one that does *not* show up on the financial models—is not simply whether the withdrawal rate you choose will work over a 30-plus-year period but also how those annual withdrawals will make you *feel*.

Recall this chart from the book:

Retirement Year	Actual Year	Beginning Year Balance	Withdrawal	Post Withdrawal	Return	End of Year Balance
1	1972	$1,000,000.00	$100,000.00	$900,000.00	19.15%	$1,072,350.00
2	1973	1,072,350.00	$100,000.00	$972,350.00	-15.03%	$826,205.80
3	1974	$826,205.80	$100,000.00	$726,205.80	-26.95%	$530,493.33
4	1975	$530,493.33	$100,000.00	$430,493.33	38.46%	$596,061.07
5	1976	$596,061.07	$100,000.00	$496,061.07	24.20%	$616,107.85

Appendix Figure 1

This was the sample retiree who tried to take out 10 percent of his retirement account ($100,000 per year). As we learned, at this pace, he never recovered.

Now look at this chart:

Retirement Year	Actual Year	Beginning Year Balance	Withdrawal	Post Withdrawal	Return	End of Year Balance
1	1972	$1,000,000.00	$30,000.00	$970,000.00	19.15%	$1,155,755.00
2	1973	$1,155,755.00	$30,000.00	$1,125,755.00	-15.03%	$956,554.02
3	1974	$956,554.02	$30,000.00	$926,554.02	-26.95%	$676,847.71

Appendix Figure 2

This retiree *is* following the recommended safe withdrawal rate. She's withdrawing just 3 percent of her original $1 million retirement fund; $30,000 a year. At this withdrawal rate, her retirement plan *does* make it 30 years.

But think about the stress this retiree is undergoing in the early years of her retirement. Her portfolio is down more than 30 percent in year *three.*

Imagine this was your retirement. You are *already* following the safe withdrawal rate, taking out the minimum amount, but it feels like your retirement house is on fire. You will be wondering, what comes next? An up year? Another down year?

The point is that along with the quantitative side of the safe withdrawal rate, there is also the *qualitative* side—the component of your retirement plan that factors in your own levels of stress and happiness. This will never show up in charts.

Even the recommended 3 percent involves some risk, and there are times when the stress may be just too much to handle.

In planning your retirement, it is important to work with someone who has expertise in many different options and is open to solutions from *both* the financial and insurance worlds.

I would be honored to help you continue the journey of discovery. Learn how to take advantage of the Fifth Option.

For a free, no obligation 20-minute phone consultation, call me at 206.683.3375.

Or visit our website to book an appointment: **Waltercyoung3.com**
I look forward to working with you!

—Walter C. Young III, MBA, RICP

INTERESTED IN BRINGING A FINANCIAL PRESENTATION TO YOUR GROUP?

Peter G. Bielagus has delivered over 1,000 presentations to universities, corporations, associations, and the United States Military. He has spoken in 49 states and 8 countries and has even been flown out to military ships at sea to present to servicemembers. He would welcome the chance to work with your group.

For more information about working with Peter,
please visit **www.peterbspeaks.com**.

NOTES

CHAPTER 5

1. Aaron O'Neill, "Life expectancy in the United States, 1860–2020," Statista, February 3, 2021, https://www.statista.com/statistics/1040079/ life-expectancy-united-states-all-time/#:~:text=Over%20the%20past%20 160%20years,to%2078.9%20years%20in%202020.

2. Seattle Times staff, "A brief history of retirement: It's a modern idea," December 31, 2013, https://www.seattletimes.com/ nation-world/a-brief-history-of-retirement-its-a-modern-idea/.

3. Liz Davidson, "The History of Retirement Benefits," Workforce, June 21, 2016, https://www.workforce.com/news/the-history-of-retirement-benefits#:~:text=In%201875%2C%20The%20American%20 Express,employers%20in%20the%20United%20States.

4. Sarah Laskow, "How Retirement Was Invented," *The Atlantic*, October 24, 2014, https://www.theatlantic.com/business/archive/2014/10/how-retirement-was-invented/381802/#:~:text=In%20the%20United%20 States%2C%20starting,Company%20started%20offering%20private%20 pensions.&text=Most%20of%20these%20pension%20programs%20 pegged%20the%20retirement%20age%20to%2065.

5. Vauhini Vara, "The Real Reason for Pensions," *New Yorker*, December 4, 2013, https://www.newyorker.com/business/currency/ the-real-reason-for-pensions.

6. Workplace Flexibility 2010, Georgetown University Law Center, "A Timeline of the Evolution of Retirement in the United States," (2010), https://scholarship.law.georgetown.edu/cgi/viewcontent. cgi?article=1049&context=legal.

7. Ibid.

8. Social Security History, "Life Expectancy for Social Security," Social Security Administration, https://www.ssa.gov/history/lifeexpect.html.

9. Frequently Asked Questions, "Age 65 Retirement," Social Security Administration, https://www.ssa.gov/history/age65.html.

10. Workplace Flexibility 2010, Georgetown University Law Center, "A Timeline of the Evolution."

11. Ibid.

CHAPTER 7

1. Readers should be aware that we used Investopedia as a source because it is a widely accessible resource. In addition, readers and investors should be aware that S&P historical returns can be different. Some calculations exclude dividends or do not adjust for inflation. While the data can be different, the overall message is the same. It is the *randomness* of the sequence that creates the wild swings in returns.

CHAPTER 8

1. Sam would be 1.7 million in debt because for 17 years he would have to borrow $100,000 per year from someone—kids, grandkids, etc.

2. Some retirees will have income from interest, rents, and dividends. But for many this will not be enough, and they will be forced to liquidate parts of their portfolio each year.

3. Wade D. Pfau and Michael Finke, "Integrating Whole Life Insurance into a Retirement Income Plan: Emphasis on Cash Value as a Volatility Buffer Asset," Wealth Building Cornerstones, April 2019, https://retirementincomejournal.com/wp-content/uploads/2020/03/WBC-Whitepaper-Integrating-Whole-Life-Insurance-into-a-Retirement-Income-Plan-Emphasis-on-Cash-Value-as-a-Volatility-Buffer-Asset.pdf.

CHAPTER 9

1. Jack Willoughby, "Did Investors Learn Anything from 2008's Crash?" *Barron's*, July 24, 2010, https://www.barrons.com/articles/SB50001424052 9702035878045753790633031963 10?tesla=y.

2. John O'Toole, "Your Portfolio Has More Risk Than You Think," *Forbes*, November 4, 2015, https://www.forbes.com/sites/randywarren/2015/11/04/ your-portfolio-has-more-risk-than-you-think/?sh=7dfb550453c2.

3. You do have to remember to consult your advisor to ensure your withdrawal strategy is correct to keep the tax-free status. You probably will need a mix of withdrawals and loans to achieve your goals, and your policy has to stay in force to avoid taxes.

CHAPTER 11

1. Although advisors use the retirement danger zone frequently, Dr. Wade Pfau, professor of retirement income at the American College of Financial Services, has a wonderfully detailed view of the risks of a down market just before and after retirement. He can be found at retirementresearcher.com.

2. THE BUCKET PLAN is a registered trademark of C2P Capital Advisory Group, LLC, and is used with permission. The Bucket Plan Graphic is Copyright © 2009 by C2P Capital Advisory Group, LLC. All rights reserved. No part of this publication may be reproduced, distributed, or transmitted in any form or by any means, including photocopying, recording, or other electronic or mechanical methods, without the prior written permission of the C2P Capital Advisory Group, LLC.

CHAPTER 13

1. To be fair, some pensions are underfunded and have even failed. A pension's payout ability is based upon the financial strengths and claims-paying ability of the provider.

2. Often the gap between payout options is not this large. We have used this example to easily demonstrate the concept of pension maximization.

3. The numbers in this chapter are for demonstration purposes only. Actual numbers will vary, depending on the particular pension. With many of today's pensions, the difference between the life-only option and the survivorship options is not as great as illustrated in this chapter. However, even though the gap may be narrower, when viewed over a lifetime, several hundred thousand dollars can still be at stake. Therefore it is worth the exercise for a pensioner and their spouse to go through the Pension Max process.

4. Even if the premiums of the life insurance policy were higher than the extra income received from the life-only option, many pensioners still elected to use a life insurance policy to maximize their pension. By having the life-only option with a life insurance policy, they not only receive the highest guaranteed income, they also have flexibility and legacy.

CHAPTER 14

1. All guarantees are backed by the credit worthiness of the insurance company. Make sure you do your research about the financial strength of the company. The major rating agencies are a good place to start.

2. There are many other kinds of annuities, but for simplicity, we are only looking at the SPIA option. Consult your advisor to review all of your choices.

3. SPIA distribution rates depend on current economic factors and the age of the SPIA owner. For illustration purposes, we have chosen to use 7 percent as the distribution rate, based on historical factors. Current rates might be higher or lower at the time of reading. It is important to get multiple quotes when purchasing a SPIA.

4. All guarantees are backed by the credit worthiness of the insurance company. Make sure you do your research about the financial strength of the company. The major rating agencies are a good place to start.

CHAPTER 15

1. SPIA distribution rates depend on current economic factors and the age of the SPIA owner. For illustration purposes, we have chosen to use 7 percent as the distribution rate, based on historical factors. Current rates might be higher or lower at the time of reading. It is important to get multiple quotes when purchasing a SPIA.

CHAPTER 16

1. There are annuities that have inflation protection built in, and they can be part of any personal retirement considerations.

CHAPTER 17

1. The guarantee is based on the financial strength and claims-paying ability of the insurance company. Tax-free withdrawals are possible through a combination of withdrawals and loans. The policy must remain in force. Please consult your advisor for additional information.

ABOUT THE AUTHORS

Walter C. Young III, MBA, RICP, is president of One Strategic Capital, a 401(k) and financial planning firm in Bainbridge, Washington. He began his career in the financial services industry in the early 1990s, working for a portfolio and 401(k) advisor in San Francisco. After earning his MBA, Walter took a break from financial services and worked for Deloitte Consulting. There he began to see that corporate strategies implemented by the best run corporations emphasized reducing overall risk and opportunity cost, while maximizing cash flow for shareholder value. He immediately realized that individual households would benefit greatly by the same strategies. If individual households have a cash-flow focus, the efficiencies they gain may very well determine their financial success.

Since that time, Walter has developed a signature approach that puts these lessons at the forefront of strategies for individuals and small business owners. His blend of individual and corporate experience has produced a unique way at looking at an individual's financial situation. He begins every relationship with the same question: "If you were a business, would you invest in you?"

Walter has become a specialist in economic-based planning theory and a thought leader, helping clients develop a cash-flow-centric strategy that helps them have better retirement income streams. Walter is an industry speaker, both nationally and internationally, as well as a trainer, panel advisor, and recipient of numerous awards. He has served on the board of advisors for industry systems and is a regular contributor to the advancement of cash-flow-centric planning modules. Walter is married with three children and lives in the Seattle area. He enjoys traveling, running, and being an active member in his community.

Peter G. Bielagus (pronounced Bill-a-gus) has been an author and a professional speaker for more than 15 years. He has written three books on personal finance, including his most recent book, *Why Bother: How the Worst Pickup Line of My Life Changed My Financial Future and How It Can Change Yours Too.*

He has delivered more than 1,000 speeches on money management to college, corporate, and military audiences. Peter has spoken in 49 states (all except Alaska) and eight countries. He has even given presentations on military ships at sea.

Peter's past clients include the United States Military, Zappos.com, and Harvard Law School. A frequent guest of the media, Peter has appeared in the *Wall Street Journal*, *USA Today*, and the *Miami Herald*. He even has his own YouTube series, "Money in the Movies," which is a personal finance show that uses popular movies to teach financial lessons.

He lives in Portsmouth, New Hampshire.